WHEN DIVAS LAUGH:
The Diva Squad Poetry Collective

edited by

Chezia Thompson Cager

An Imprint of Black Classic Press

When Divas Laugh: The Diva Squad Poetry Collective. Copyright © 2001. Chezia Thompson Cager, Editor. All rights reserved. Printed in the United States of America. No part of this book may be copied or circulated in any printed or electronic format without the written permission of the copyright holder.

For information, address Black Classic Press, P.O. Box 13414, Baltimore, Maryland 21203.

Photographs by Expressly Portraits Photography.

Design by Trish Cerbelli.

Some of the poems in this volume have appeared in the following publications: *Articulate Contemporary Art Review, The Baltimore Sun's* Web site, SunSpot.net, BMa: The Sonya Sanchez Literary Magazine, *Baltimore Writer's Alliance Newsletter,* the "Carl Clark: Photographer" catalogue—Maryland Art Place, *Dancing Shadow Review, Function at the Junction Anthology, Jambalaya Magazine, Poetry Baltimore, New Breezes: An Anthology of African American Literary Voices, Quintessence, Rhapsody In Black,* the Joyce Scott catalogue for "Kicking It With the Old Masters"—Baltimore Museum of Art, *The Afro-American Newspaper, The Maryland Poetry Review, New Voices: Trinidad & Tobago, Obsidian II: Black Literature in Review, The Pearl, Thy Mother's Glass I, Village Views, Word Up Baltimore* CD, and *WordWrights Magazine.*

Published by Inprint Editions, an imprint of Black Classic Press.

First Inprint Editions paperback published 2001.

ISBN 1-58073-031-0

I wish to express my thanks for the Maryland State Arts Council's support, in the form of the 1999 Individual Artist's Award in Poetry. Without their help, this book would not have been possible.

*This book is dedicated to the Women and the Men
who pushed us forward into our mutual destinies.*

Axe

The Diva Squad Poetry Collective

PROLOGUE 8

I. INCURSION CYCLE:
LENETT NEFERTITI ALLEN—
MY MOTHER GAVE ME MUSIC... 9

My Mother Gave Me Music 10
Why A Lazy Woman Loathes Leaving Her Bed 12
Untitled 13
Because 15
Sunday Morning Orange Juice 16
I AM A Mansion 18
In My Sista's House 20
A Maze Groove 21
A Call To Action On A New Day Dawning For Naomi 22
Mother African Dance 23
Some People In My Life *(Like Lacy)* 25
Dania 26
A Prelude To A Time 27
Spaces 28
When All Else Fails, Write Him A Poem 29
While We Wait 30
Fishin' 32
The Women Gather *(for Asantewa)* 34
Ode To The Spoken Word Weavas & Divas 35
Cherish the Times 36

II. ATROPHY CYCLE:
LINDA JOY BURKE—NICK OF TIME... 37

Breakfast on 12th Street 38
These Are Some of My Blues 39
Untitled 41
This Is Why I Remember King 42
Grateful for Shelter: Leaving Otterbein 45
Driving at the Speed of Life 46
Nick of Time 47
Artificial Light 49
Lethargy 51
Leaving Suburbia 52
Warnings: Los Angeles Riots 53
For Carlotta Who Died at the Age of 20 54
Afrikaner—Part I *(The Famine)* 55
Too Cool Reflections on the Double Digit Double Helix 57
The Peace Poem 59
On Becoming An Artist 60
Nosy Lady Lament 62

III. DESTRUCTION CYCLE:
JAKI-TERRY—DRIVE BY SHOOTINGS... 63

To Understand Is to Understand 64

Perceptions	65
I Wanna Tell My Babies	66
Untitled #1002	67
Conditions	68
In Search of Rainbows	69
Before We Heal	70
Truth Don't Need A Name	71
Leo Sun, Scorpio Moon, Cancer…Rising–1	72
Miami Beach	73
1994	76
Song #222	77
Poinsettias	78
Conversation	79
Peacock	80
Abstract	81
His Eyes Talk	82
7 Years Later…	83
A Ghetto Girl's Love Song	84
Ode To Weequaic Heights	85
Sometimes It Ain't All About Sex	86
Then There Are Times…	87
Psalms 139:14	88

IV. REJUVENATION CYCLE:
CHEZIA THOMPSON CAGER–TAKING IT TO THE STREETS   89

Under Flower: The 1983 March On Washington	90
La Fleur Haitienne	91
Forbidden Fruit	92
MLK	93
La Danse Du Dragon	94
A Black History Month Poem	96
House Made of Dawn	97
I Thought He Was A Plant	98
Chanson D'amour Creole	99
A Date With Destiny	102
Alien Pussy	103
JFK, Jr.'s Last Flight	105
La Femme du Dragon: A Choreopoem	106
The Daughter Chronicles: Things Her Bad Butt Did	107
Return To Goree: Or The Bride	108
Sound Haiku: 5–7–5	111
Joyce Scott Haiku	112
The Eye of Carl Clark: A Photopoem	113
Psalm To What Is Spiritual In Each Of Us	115

INDEX OF POEMS BY SUBJECT MATTER   116

THE AUTHORS   119

PROLOGUE

You Sweep The Floor
By Jelaluddin Balkhi or Rumi *(meaning Roman Anatolia*)*

"The lord of beauty enters the soul
as a man walks into an orchard
in Spring.
        Come into me
that way again!
                Light the lamp
in the eye of Joseph. Cure Jacob's
sadness. Though you never left,
come and sit down here and ask,
"Why are you so confused?"

Like a fresh idea in an artist's mind,
you fashion things before they come into being.

You sweep the floor like the man
who keeps the doorway.
                When you brush
a form clean, it becomes
what it truly is.

You guard your silence perfectly
like a water bag that doesn't leak.

You live where Shams lives,
because your heart-donkey was strong enough
to take you there."

                      Interpreted translation by Coleman Barks
                      from *The Essential Rumi* (with thanks
                      for his permission to reprint poem)

*Rumi—born September 30, 1207 in Balkh, Afghanistan,
died December 17, 1273 in Konya, Turkey.

Lenett Nefertiti Allen

1. Incursion Cycle:
My Mother Gave Me Music

"...
You don't have to prove to me
You're beautiful to strangers
I've got loving eyes of my own
and I can tell...
        You belong to me..."

"You Belong To Me" by Carly Simon, Michael McDonald,
sung on *Rhythm of Love* CD by Anita Baker.

My Mother Gave Me Music

initially the drum,
the bridge between two worlds,
her womb and the one waiting to receive me
with extended hands.

She would sing me lullabies
learned from her mother who
learned them from her mother who
learned them from church,
play me 45s on the box with little colored disks
that made the Platters and the Drifters fit
around the spinning sound of doo-wops,
and albums on the new hi-fi that she would buy
to teach me jazz by sight and sound
the names and notes of
Ramsey's wading, Nancy's guessing
Cannonball's Mercy, Ray's gotta woman;
and the only white woman in the stacks
made me smile inside
whenever she sang about *People*.

On occasion she would take me uptown where
a little blind boy named Stevie played *Fingertips*;
Mary Wells, Miracles, Martha & the Vandellas,
Marvelettes, Marvin Gaye, Supremes, Temptations
and The 4 Tops gave us a Royal Theater show
while James Brown called on "Maceo"
and the Fabulous Flames crooned on
"Baby, please don't go."

She would pretty me up with ribbons and bows
and take me to the dinner shows,
first at a club called Venus where I first saw
a man on silver crutches and wondered
if he was a prince or a duke
'cause they called him "Sir Walter Jackson,"
and nobody ate when he sang.

Later downtown at the Playboy Club,
we would laugh at all the
bunny butts switchin' around
as Lionel Hampton made these sounds
I never heard before on the xylophone/chimes
(not like they taught us in school),
and I learned from Billy Eckstein
how different music could feel
when you listened with your eyes closed.

Down the road she would turn me onto
radio stations playing serious jazz,
late night TV music shows,
news of who was coming town,
and the latest addition to her CD collection,
all the while listening for
what was good about folk like
Seal, Yoni, Bonnie Rait, and George Michael's latest,
blowing me away every time with her
perfect sense of perception.

But that was all to come.

You see, my mother gave me music,
initially the drum,
her heart to which I cling now
listening for her breathing me a wind song
"Sweetie, don't cry"
as the doctor stands with extended hands
waiting to weight me in at birth.

WHY A LAZY WOMAN LOATHES LEAVING HER BED

As the world turns resplendent
she is profoundly moved
Awakened to dawn's moist and dampened dew
her vaginal gleanings gather to sepia petal
and pistol sweetly 'surrected
Touching wondrously the velvety wonders of
skin and hair, blood and muscle, rhythm and pulse
beneath her quivering tide

She questions to rise
lest she spills forth to flood the sphere
but rather lie there prone and pregnant
within the fullness of her own aromatic flesh
to touch, to taste, to penetrate creation's womb
'til evolution comes round
each cyclical hour's passing
comes with dusk's meandering clouds
comes with night as ebony shroud
then comes no more

She is fulfilled, profoundly moved
as the world awaits
a woman's touch

UNTITLED

Who am i?
i thought i was a woman 'til i woke up this morning
and couldn't feel myself, couldn't even see myself in the mirror
i must have dreamed myself out of existence last night
when i beat the shit out of that tree with a hammer
to the point of exhaustion, bleeding anger all over the ground
soaked down to the roots

i looked up at the tree to say
"Asante sana, sista, for letting me vent"
She dropped a peach into my mouth
and i ate myself alive with such viciousness
my teeth were jarred loose
i buried the pit and core of me so far into the ground
my fingers bled
What was left of me crawled backwards on all 4's
into the reality of my phone ringing
Nemi asked, "How are you?"
I burst into tears, "I need more sleep"
and went back to the dream
covered in peach blood dirt juice

A drum fell out the sky, but my fingers were numb
so I played it with my forehead
remembering Babtunde's words, "The drum can talk. . .it talks"
that's when I gave up the ghost to
Jesus, Geronimo and the drum
banging out rhythms with a purple-blue bruised forehead

Somebody, please

  speak to me
  i give up wanting to be defined
  speak my name
  i give up wanting to be a mother
  speak to me
  i give up wanting to be a lover
  speak my name
  i give up wanting
  speak to me
  i give up
  and just pulsate

swollen female essence
the significant other than this uterus of mine
which i welcome and embrace
especially when my moon comes down
in the middle of the night

BECAUSE

I could be next to him again
beside the place where he leaves and returns
at will / because he knows he can
if he knew he could

I sit with Marvin Gaye on a continuous loop
I want you over and over and over again
from inside that place where
aching hearts are compelled to bleed

this is the way love goes after
a million minutes of madness
listening for the logic in the music
coming from that same place
way far deep inside me where
he still lives sometimes and sings me insanity
from that place where
everything healthy and sane
ceases to exist beyond logic / because
I breathe, therefore, I feel
he hurts, therefore, he hurts
this is the way of a Trouble Man

he use to place his head inside my hand
and breathe love that surpasses all understanding
because / he loves that way I remember
how we sat in his back yard under trees
reading each other's poetry
from that place where I now crumble and crack
this hard exterior stoic grief / because
we are the choices we make
long after the music makes no sense

but, he does and he can
if he only knew he could again
this is the way love goes
rising to the occasion of dawn
on a continuous loop of madness

SUNDAY MORNING ORANGE JUICE

God crept in on me
like She do on Sunday mornings
performing miracles, saying
>   *Be rid of your blues*
and I shouted
>   *Hallelujah—stop the madness*
I'm getting off right here
where I've been delivered
a black woman onto the streets of
my time has come to jump up
be free of the boogyman
leap like naked spirit defying
time, space, gravity
dance straight to my new address
is The Universe

People peering from cars and windows
will wonder
>   *What's gotta hold of that chil'*
while a child is sure to ask me
why I cut oranges horizontally
I'll tell him
>   *Honey, you gotta cut life right*
>   *at an angle where you can*
>   *suck the living daylights out it*
I'll help him gather seeds falling from his mouth
so he won't miss any opportunity
to sprout nourishing dreams

And I KNOW
some man is sure to look up my dress
while I'm gathering seeds
trying to walk me to my woman temple
Imagine us trying to keep time step
while he's marching toward American born
African self actualization
and I'm doing this Samba to the tune of
womanhood's primordial screams
Brotha please
I want to spotlight this dance solo

for real, I need

deep wet long succulent tender
kisses by moonlight
and to lay my thigh across your back
while my sleeping foot caresses your love
But I've got to get to me
and this entire trip is chartered
woMINE

Tell you what...

when you've shed your scales of
ghetto leaches and racist parasites
and I've exhausted this repertoire of
evolutionary rhythmic movements
maybe then we can settle into the
black womaness-maness
of a new Sunday morning
and drink orange juice together

I AM A MANSION

with 2 wings, split levels, multi levels
Lots of cozy nooks and crannies
A little spacey in places
Bright, breezy, charming
Downright homey, if you will
Illuminated from within by
blazing fires, natural light
Wired for sound, cable TV and
up to 5 billion watts of raw electrical input

I AM A mansion
a tower of power standing strong in the face of
storms, natural and unnatural disasters
Built on solid ground, on sacred ground
Ancient spirits sometimes visit to sing, dance, chant
and laugh at nothing in particular
except during full moon when they speak in tongue

I AM A mansion
made of natural materials
Mahogany, cherry, ebony, stone
None of that synthetic stuff here
Designed with strong lines, natural curves, interesting angles
From any view, a sublime structure

I AM A mansion
well kept through time
Age has not withered the façade
beckoning all to enter, but be forewarned
The carpet has fingers
and the floors get damp when it rains outside

I AM A mansion
or more accurately, a womansion
not for sale, but up for rent and
always looking for a good long-term tenant
These are the rules—
There will be no tearing down of walls nor
any exterior alterations made whatsoever
Take it or leave it as is

Malicious destruction and defacing of the property
are cause for immediately eviction
And don't even think about
bringing nothing tacky up in here
'cause you see,
I am not your typical dwelling

I AM A mansion

IN MY SISTA'S HOUSE

Coffee and cornbread with marmalade glaze
mangoes and melons, magenta red grapes,
garden plucked roses with dew scented leaves,
music Mahalia to hearken the day.
The glory of morning is grace at her table;
kitchen is temple in my sista's house.

Closets with secrets and hand-me-down gifts,
Grandmother's hair pins to wear in my locks,
scratchy worn albums recalling old dances,
tea party laughter crescendos 'til dusk.
Hours pass swiftly unnoticed in shadows;
time has new meaning in my sista's house.

Fireside readings from books and new poems,
snuggled beneath an old quilt side by side,
loved ones remembered in family stories,
cook outs and picnics, the joys of our youth.
In moonlight we notice the signs of our aging;
gray hair is honored in my sista's house.

Window breeze blowing a sandalwood scent,
candlelight softens the room all aglow,
words spoken softly, sweet dreams they inspire,
her lap is my pillow to slumber 'til morn.
A prayer she whispers for nothing to harm me;
peace be still softly in my sista's house.

Last minute kisses on foreheads and noses,
smiles through our tears we brush gently aside,
one final picture to capture the moment,
waving long after she fades out of view.
And I am the better for all that she gives me
whenever I visit my sista's house.

A MAZE GROOVE
(for Frankie Beverly & Maze)

There's only so much you can do in a kitchen
to ease your worried bones
At some point outside calls
That's where you find yourself
inside a paradise green
sprinkled pink with bougainvillea blossoms
and fauna fanning a tropical breeze
You find yourself
giving praise on the pulse of a sacred river
right outside your door
where tears come naturally
'cause its natural to be filled with joy
and "thank you" is a prayer
You find yourself
learning the language of lizards in trees
that speak in elder tongue
standing firm in truth
and everything around you has a lesson to tell
You find yourself
smiling as easy as
sun shines cross your face
and grace finds the faithful
those who believe in believing
And suddenly
the job doesn't matter
the bills don't matter
the lover who won't act right doesn't matter
not even tomorrow matters
'cause you have today
this one, glorious, awesome day when
you find yourself
waving at boaters passing by
like life ain't nothing but a
Maze kind of happy feeling
And all is well, is well in your soul
And all is well in your soul

A CALL TO ACTION ON A NEW DAY DAWNING FOR NAOMI
(a woman friend mugged in broad daylight)

No more.
No more shall we stand helplessly by while
our sistas are being abused.
No more shall we depend on police protection
when violent crimes against women rise
to epidemic proportions.
We shall fashion ourselves the colors of fire,
the new uniform of revolutionary women
with a kick ass agenda for the 21st century.
We shall sharpen our spears, check our razors and guns,
synchronize our watches and do street patrol 24-7
in Zulu battle formation.
We shall boot dance our way across country
wearing signs that say
I HAVE PMS AND A GUN—ANY QUESTIONS?
We shall collar all the new jack wanna be b-boys
to the point of strangulation every time the word bitch
even feels like it's coming out of their mouths,
then kidnap all the b-girls who wanna be boys
and turn them over to Olufunmilayo for a
90 day intensive non-stop African dance class
culminating in a Rites of Passage ceremony
to be held way deep in the bush of central Africa.
We shall respond to every desperate scream and call for help
wherever gang rapes, beatings and senseless murders occur
to cleanse the earth of filth and slime once and for all.
We shall run a military coup, take over women's penitentiaries
and free those women doing time for self-defense related murder,
then raid the White House and starve the president
until he signs all official pardons.
We shall petition the world court to free every woman
held hostage by sexist governments and religions,
and if the world won't listen
we shall hold an international boycott on sex
until the patriarchal regime surrenders
to the power of pussy.
And when our work is done
we shall hold council atop Mount Pele,
sing a sweet song of freedom,
and study war
no more.

MOTHER AFRICAN DANCE
(for Olufunmilayo)

Dancers were merely dancers to me
graceful girls, pretty and pleasing to watch
'til I saw Olu bring a full grown woman
to the floor
to the dance
and I knew
I had never really known dancing before

Mother threw down

flashing rhythms with the sway of her hips
oozing grace with the turn of her wrists
holding court with the countenance of her stance
giving up much quick step
coming down solid on the beat every time
She made the walls tremble
the ground rumble
unfilled spaces her personal domain
And then had the nerve to

pause a profile

long enough for
brothas to catch their breath
and sistas to check their dos

She had just begun

gyrating muscles like ripples on a stream
shaking and writhing like a she-thing possessed
teaching more history with an arch of her back
than 15 scholars could preach in a day
pointing the way to the Motherland
with an outstretched thunder thigh
perfectly extended for effect
Olu! Olu!
the African dance Aesthetic
in the flesh

I remember sitting there
on the front row wishing

I wanna learn how to *mooooove* like her
learn from the beat of her drum
be embraced by all that spirit
feel that radiant smile directed at me
for a step well done
one day when I grow up to the dance
and I knew
I had never really known
what it was to be a woman

Years later
with half a century under her gele
she's still throwin' down
holding court
holding class
making music
teaching and preaching
giving and living
being an institution all her own
the pulse of our community
sunshine draped in Oshun hues
another too often undersung shero

Meanwhile
I'm still trying to get it
how she *mooooooves* like that

and because of Olu
I now overstand why
dancing is vital to growth

SOME PEOPLE IN MY LIFE
(Like Lacy)

Some people in my life
stay with me always

The things they say are
as clear as
the silence I hear
when they aren't there

The things they do are
constantly happening
in my private laughter

The comfort they give is
felt in being content
with this life God hands me
when they are gone

Some people in my life
never leave

DANIA

moved into the studio across the hall
She reminds me of someone who knows things
but refuses to tell all
She paints
Her subjects
male lovers
in various holding positions
from ceiling to floor
She uses oils and acrylics
Something smells like pain in there

She smiles a pretty hello
We talk / sometimes share stories about
our sexual exploits with younger men
Her logic is so pure, so to the point
Tie them up, gag them, get yours first, and go
She knows things

The other day
she moved
whereabouts unknown
I miss her a lot
I miss her art
Mostly I miss
all those things about her
I never, ever intended to know

A PRELUDE TO A TIME

For a few brief moments
they play sweet seduction games
with fingers and sweaty palms
and hands entwined
A prelude to a time of

tasting each other
and licking away the loneliness
'til the next day
and the day after that
and yet another when
finally their lips cease to resonate
with wordless sounds
They say goodbye and

move on to their other lives
occasionally looking over their shoulders
for the person they met
and loved
and dared to dance
along the razor's edge

SPACES

I.
We fill our empty spaces
with everything we own
buy all the things
we think we need
until
there's no room left
for the things
we say we want
and wonder why
love only comes
to visit

II.
THE ROOM FIRST TREMBLES
       then rumbles
     then   quakes
furniture s l i d e s across the floor
       windows rattttttttle
            glasses
          br
               eak
walls   move   in   position
    ceilings BULGE
    and suddenly
     the electricity dies

Hell hath no fury
like a woman alone
crying in the dark

WHEN ALL ELSE FAILS, WRITE HIM A POEM

Falling in love
like autumn leaves to earth
is no less a sin than
nature yielding to the cycle of death.
All are forgiven.   Surely,

I, like the sycamore and oak,
am full of God, relentlessly giving
piece by piece, even when there's nothing left,
the bare essential standing naked
exposed to winter, or worse, each other.

Tell me, where is the crime? The dive to despair
or the heart's truest urge to ascend?   Touch me,

take my hand in fearless flight above
our piles of scattered scars and decomposed kisses,
our innocence, our original smile
when once we were green and spring
could never come too soon.
But I am brown now, really brown
burnt sienna auburn golden hued,
feeling autumn an emotion as deep as darkened tomb,
waiting resurrection by fire of your flesh where
all are born between these aching thighs.   Come,

die with me, beloved, in sinless death.
I am the light, the way,
the Tao of your burdened soul,

and I shall render you a rose in June.

WHILE WE WAIT

for that special someone to beam down
atom by precious atom
smack in the middle of
right here, right now where
hair stands up on the back of our necks
sweat pours down our shivering thighs
spit drools down our quivering lips
nipples stand erect
buttocks flex involuntary
and words turn in to sound like ooooooooo…

While we wait
on that streetcar named desire to
crash through our front door
on the strength of a thousand
462 horse powered cylinder Lamborghini engines
racing into eternity

While we wait
we learn to call on Mercy and peace be still

We learn to treat ourselves to healthy doses of
love you back in the mirror morning, noon and night
We learn how to be warriors of the heart
doing a Jenny Keith walk like samurai on a mission to
a Luther Vandross love song
We learn how to pamper ourselves with
long, luxurious bubble baths
scented oils, silk underthings
2 fingers of Remy VSOP or
imported Indian spice tea
whatever we prefer because it's our life
and we call the shots
We learn how to sleep alone and like it / sometimes
It's better than sleeping with
body by Fisher / brain by Mattel
no matter how tall, tan, scintillating, tantalizing
or seemingly intelligent second best looks
We learn how to deal with our aloneness
and to treasure silence as a sacred space

to be our own best companion
the person with whom we most enjoy spending time
We learn how to see God in all things
including ourselves
knowing we are precious jewels
and whoever didn't get us to didn't deserve us anyway

While we wait
we learn above all to
trust the divine order of life
never looking back, always looking forward to
the day, the way, the when, the how
love will surely come

And while we wait
sometimes it's necessary
to call on Mercy and peace be still

FISHIN

I.
My father tried to teach me fishin
I preferred crabs
I s'pose there's a sport to it
Idol talkin
Lazy lipsincin
Meditatin on reeds and rushes
Contemplatin bait
Waitin
Bein still
Bein quiet
Jes bein
Which is why I s'pose
fishin is more art than game

II.
It must be huge
Doggon rod's bendin at a 45 degree angle
less, man says, *"That's a turtle down there."*
Course, I'm thinkin—or a dead somebody
So then, man hands the rod over to the boy and tells 'im
"Don't try to reel it in or you'll snap the line."
Dontcha know soon as he turn his back
that fool boy commence to reelin
Well, mind my business, I most certainly won't
This is the most excitin thing I've seen
in a whole month of Sundays
"Hey boy," I says, *"watcha think it is?"*
Boy's eyebrows shoot straight up in his head
"Somethin big," he's guessin, *"Must be a turtle."*
Course, I know it's somebody dead as dirt
After all, this is Miami Beach

Durin full moon, folk take to bridges
like white on rice
Crabbin, shrimpin, makin offerins to the sea—
oranges and melons, indiscreet packages
reeled down to Cigarette speed boat motorists below
Two pole pros loungin in beach chairs
rod in one hand, beer in the other
radios blastin cubana samba

with a second rod perched on the rail
wedged against the pedestrian curb
purposely impeding the path of bikers en route
Course, I don't mind walkin cross the bridge tonight
Everything's so quiet, freeway traffic notwithstandin
After all, this is Miami Beach

So then, man finally stops diggin in his cooler for
God only knows what—an extra hand I s'pose—
and comes up with a thing-a-ma-jig
"Somethin to reinforce the line," he tells the boy
Well, roun bout 2 A.M. they still tryin to figure out
the most delicate way to reel up   ...Jaws?
"Wish ya'll luck," I says
headin my bike for home
in search of another adventure

See, that's the problem with me

I don't have much patience for fishin
while these folk, on the other hand
do it all the time
at least every full moon
and who knows how long they'll be there
debatin over what kind of turtle it is
if that's what it is
Course, I'm still thinkin Luca Brazzi
which is why, I s'pose
fishin is more science than sport

   III.
I am my father's daughter
forever his adventure seeking girl.

THE WOMEN GATHER
(for Asantewa)

The stretch and curves of Dogwood Road
would have us believe we have traveled far
beyond the line of demarcation.
Yet not so far away
our city sleeps. Hereford snores.
No one hears us split the night with ancient tongue~
Mdupe, mdupe Ogun, mdupe.
No one sees us lace the trail
to wooded glen, to lodge.
None but night hawk, deer and star will ever know
We are stardust, we are golden, we are filled...
Here below Grandmother Moon's delicious glow,
it is she who calls us;
calls us to harvest, fire and wood,
calls us to ritual, story and stone,
to pray and sing, to cry and sweat
our earthly Mother's womb.
We have traveled far, we daughters of Africa,
descendents of these Turtle Island shores,
so far to rediscover where we belong.
Somehow, we remember

we are more than concrete, more than
where we work and dwell, more than
statistics, battered, martyr, shrew
...and we've got to get ourselves back to the garden*
Somehow, we recall

a river runs through Dickey Hill.
And so the woman gather,
dripping morningscape with dampened loins,
with skirts perfumed in smoking ash
from lodge to hilly bank, then onto Cherry Hill
in search of water,
seeding soil with sweet,
cleansing stream with pure conviction
and dreams on out to sea,
across this town,
this Baltimore.

*Taken from "Woodstock," by Crosby, Stills, Nash & Young.

ODE TO THE SPOKEN WORD WEAVAS & DIVAS

We are the ones who deliva the word
who deliva the funk in yo face / in yo ear
Do ya hear? Do ya know?
Oh, say can YOU see
a new beat generation
spoken word rhythm nation
getting off on / getting down on
the one/ too true uncut
uncompromisin webster

We are the ones who deliva the word
who deliva the news, the views, the vibe
the reel show n tell comin atcha live
Film at 6 / story at 11
Catch us if you can / can groove
with a renegade tribe of
weavas and divas gone buck wild on
syncopated syntax and
3D rastafied pentameter

We are the ones who deliva the word
who deliva the hopes, the dreams, the visions
of a new day dawning when
all God's chil ens' gotta voice / a choice to
STAND UP / SPEAK OUT / BE HEARD / BE BOP/ BE
whatever yo mouth says yo brain can conceive cuz

silence =
silence =

and nothin said / nothin heard
nothin heard / nothin changed
nothin changed / nothin new
it's up to you and you and you too
STAND UP / SPEAK OUT / BE HEARD / BECAUSE

We are the ones who deliva the word
who deliva tomorrow's salvation

CHERISH THE TIMES

we shared here,
and tell the children
we sat in the company of great poets,
gifted writers, those who would be heard;
for surely everyone has
something worth saying,
and the blessing is in the listening,
the mustering of courage to stand up in a
crowed room and bare one's soul.
Tell the children
we were witnesses to magic,
the phenomena of genius,
the miracle of healing when
battered bards traded their burdens in print
for comforting hugs, encouraging words;
when newcomers on the scene stood up
for the first time and elbowed their way
into our hearts with poetry so profound,
putting the literati elite on notice
that even the unpublished among us
were worthy of respect from all of us,
and slumming out on Preston Street
definitely had its virtues.
Tell the children
we belonged to a family of wizards and weavas,
wordsmiths and divas, spanning the range of
human expression from Jaki-T to R.B. to Alan / Bob / John
Jenny / Meikil / Paul / Lasana / and Grif… R.I.P.
Regulars, irregulars, all were embraced
while the Bean man, curator of the collective
Word On Wednesday
kept the creative process holy sanctified;
and everyone knew the woman at 10 East
always had something sweet to eat
with teas for the fever to nurture our dreams;
we called her Linda the Magnificent,
Matron Saint of Poets.
And long after the 4th day of the week becomes
just another day in the life of,
tell the children
once upon a wonderful
there was Café Montage.

Linda Joy Burke

II. ATROPHY CYCLE:
    IN A NICK OF TIME...

"...
From a distance
we are instruments
marching in a common band
singing songs of hope
singing songs of joy.
These are the songs of everyman.
And God is watching us...
        From a distance"

"From A Distance" by Gold, sung by Bette Midler

BREAKFAST ON 12TH STREET

Breakfast made my daddy a champion.
It was the only meal he had control of,
until life in the times of hypertension.
He didn't serve Sugar Crisps® or
oatmeal soaked in milk though.

While mother slept,
he fried sausage and hash browns,
with sunny side up eggs and grits,
scrambled eggs, warmed applesauce,
fried flour coated scrapple,
fried French toast and ham,
fried bacon and waffles.

Daddy would go on for hours
after the last breakfast bite was taken
about hard times
that used to be an every day reality,
and future times
that might not really change for the better
and about covert betrayals of fragile trusts.

With the kitchen his turf
he waxed with bitter nostalgia
about his life as a Negro in America,
nurturing his girl children
with truths and warnings,
here he spoke freely
about not really being free.

THESE ARE SOME OF MY BLUES

I come from a time of air raid warnings
and the threat of the rocket's red glare
and who's got a bomb shelter,
and eating fish on Fridays,
and wearing hats to Sunday Mass
and praying to that omnipotent God
to please save my little ass.

I come from the James Brown time
of saying it loud
that we were black and we were
proud of our nappy headed heritage,
and so once again renamed,
of this we would sing.

I come from a dangerous time
of secrets and lies
a hand me down—violent time
of speaking only when spoken to
of *"stop crying or I'll give you
something to cry for—
take what you get
cause you got no choice"*
or opinion, or rights time,
an unforgiving time,
when children were not wise.

I come from a time of bombings
and riots and tear gas
and fire hoses and assassinations
and cities burning to the ground,
a time of evolution and confusion
and delusion that somewhere here in this America
there were streets paved with gold.
A time when children were not wise.

I come from a time when everyone
left who they thought they were

to find who they wanted to be in the first place,
amidst a world made in haste
and then laid minute by minute to waste
by the unconcerned masses.

I come from the time of
Earth shoes and Afros,
sit-ins and love-ins,
five-finger discounts
and panhandling Georgetown
musicians singing their own version
of these times got a hold of me blues.

I come from a time of long term
heart to hearts
with plants and cats
and pieces of land
that aren't really mine;
and with women who have been
mothers and sisters,
and age old kin and lovers;
and with men who have been
from the beginning
closely bled in like brothers.

I come from the time of ceaseless struggle
to keep up with the tick toque tick toque of the clock,
a time of hoarding fleeting moments
of awe and natural bliss.
I come from the time of
survival of the fittest.
I come from a time
when children were not wise.

UNTITLED

Keeping Balance
on the round orb,
is a masterful task,
to walk amongst blades of grass
as born free beings
not the shattered descendants
of ancients whose memories
are lost in the ruins
created by the deceptions
of our captors.

New memories make their way
through old ground.
Old ground gives way
to new thought
for all freed beings to walk with
towards horizons rising
out of flame and famine.
Memory survives with a new name
Hope.

THIS IS WHY I REMEMBER KING

I remember King, because
I know there's a young man
who lost his good home
and his babies
and his wife over some
crack cocaine,
and he thinks it's because
some white man down south didn't
treat him right.

I remember King
because it is no lie
that Mississippi thirty years
later is still the poorest
state in the union and
Haiti a war torn country
of freed Africans is still
the poorest country in the world.

I remember King
as I try to find
a movie that doesn't
have the picture of,
the description of
someone killing someone
else. I understand
that thirty years
later we are still more
fascinated with teaching
the ways of hurting each other
than with walking hand in hand.

I remember King
as I watch Giraldo's
midday KKK mothers
with their hooded
babies, saying with
some warped conviction
that *"we don't
hate anyone—we just want them
to stay out of **our** world."*
I remember King

when I hear the
testimony of one
arrested Campesina
in El Salvador, her
body raped and burned
and tortured relentlessly.
If they set her free
she may
go back to the same
poor campeñero, chances are she'll
escape to the other America.

I remembered King when
on his legal birthday
the debut of the "War
Theatre Desert Storm America at War"
opened to this free country,
as another president
betrayed everything King stood for.

I remembered King
when I sat in LaFayette
Park, with the police
and the homeless people
and I wondered if Bush's
bombs were the thousand
points of light he spoke of
earlier in his career.

I remember King
when some late night talk
show caller says that
*"this country is turning
into a fucking third
world"* and the DJ agrees,
and then someone else
throws out more hatred
20,000 watts of hatred
let freedom ring,
20,000 watts of. . .
I remember King when
I change the station

to something black and soulful
like I've had to run home again,
and I did run home again.

I remember King
when I look for my
self in the mirror
when I look for my
own passion, my own
power & my own
peace.
Let freedom ring
20,000 watts of
Let freedom ring.

I remember King
and all those who
came before me
to make my road easier.
I understand freedom's
not being free, and trusting
big brother still only
gets you a cursory pat
on the head.
Yet the flame still burns
and I shall not ever forget.
20,000 watts of let
freedom ring.

Martin Luther King Day 1992

GRATEFUL FOR SHELTER—LEAVING OTTERBEIN

The side walks are sweating off two days of rain
occasionally I spy bent heads of new blue Irises
their yellow centers gaping at the strangers
passing by, with not enough time
to read the signs
of a crippled black man
who limps up and down
the median strip in front of Camden yards.
Red light piles cars up
he shares his modest sign,
"will work for food,"
there is a white woman with broken glasses
holding a similar sign just a block away.

We are all rushing through to
the end of our 9-5 life,
we spend that time jockeying
for the best lane on the way home to alone
or the evening news,
or a lover never to be lost
or a love struggling to be found.
We do not interrupt the rush of the hour
with the plight of abandoned strangers.
We remain grateful for shelter.

DRIVING AT THE SPEED OF LIFE

My 86 Jetta GL
does not go 0-60 in less
than a minute—
does not have
150 watt-bass boosted
e-qued surround sound—
does not allow
me to deactivate my
car alarm and buzz open
my door from a distance,
is being edged out of it's
formerly cool though square
existence by,
hi tech, well rounded
vehicles with bumpers
that crumble and air
bags not made for
slight people and children.
My Jetta GL,
is already falling behind
the speed limit that rising,
feels like I'm doing the
putt putt of a Volkswagen bug
"feelin groovy." I'm
trying to stay with the
pack—but everyone else
is living out raceway fantasies
in those vehicles made for
the new millennium's cyberwoven
cruise controlled faster
than the speed of the
last decade pace, as they
blow past me doing 85 on 95,
challenging even my claim
to the so called slow lane.

NICK OF TIME

It is 1997 and I spy
some one's teenage boy
sitting in the bookstore
café looking at the pictures
in a copy of a firearms magazine.
His pudgy hands, stop turning pages,
when he discovers an ad detailing the
value of a slick hand held item.

It is 1969
in a grandmother's living room,
a buck-toothed, four-eyed, pre-pubescent girl,
discovers a pistol, that looks like the cowboy
guns she used to wear for play.
She grabs it up and instinctively
points it towards the couch wall.

It is 1997
and some one's child
is told that his big brother's
22 rifle is not a toy, he still
reaches out to touch it,
just a little look / see,
and for his curiosity
is accidentally shot in the belly,
and some one's child dies.

It is 1969
the bucktoothed, four-eyed, pre-pubescent girl,
doesn't think that this gun is real,
starts to pull back the hammer,
finger on the trigger;
caught in the act she
is startled into reality
just in the nick of time,
by the *"you don't know if it's a toy"*
rationalization of a sister who showed
up at the living room door.
In that nick of time,

no one died and
no one told till it was too late
for her to be punished.

It is 1997
and some one's teenage son
has been sitting in the bookstore café
for nearly an hour reading
a firearms magazine and ignoring
everything else in the room.
No one seems to know
and no one seems to care
what he will do with
these images planted there in his mind,
or who may have to distract him
from hand held destruction
just in the nick of time.

ARTIFICIAL LIGHT

She had auburn hair, they said
in the artificial light,
you really couldn't tell
how old she was,
though she did admit to remembering
being sent out of some
southern restaurant in '39
'cause she wasn't the right color.

They said, in the artificial light
she'd sit for hours
rocking back and forth
humming the same sad melody
over and over,
and if you asked her what it was
she'd shake her head,
look away as if she hadn't heard.

They said she was an
eclectic combination
of the reincarnated souls
of Hesse, Plath,
St. John of the Cross,
deeply in love,
touched by grace almost,
yet in the artificial light
without dimension and profoundly troubled.

They said in the artificial light
you couldn't see dust on her
drawn curtains.
the floors seemed suitable for company,
and in the blue lit bathroom
the truth of her most personal habits
was well concealed.
She let not sunshine fade
couch brocade,
or hint of subtle hues
in dark oriental rugs,
or hint of obvious lines
in faded sagging skin.

She'd say after days
of silently watching
her plants grow yellow
without the sun,
how much, better they were
at night
without natural light
they did not crackle when they grew.

They said she only allowed
guests to visit
in that evening's subdued light,
and though she smiled easily,
she never looked you straight in the eye,
and she asked too many questions
without waiting for the answers
or remembering what she'd said.

They said when she stopped
asking questions
and started fiddling with
lamps and light switches
that it was time to go.
When she'd sit in her chair
rocking back and forth
humming the same sad melody
over and over,
you found your own way to the door.

They said she spent
a fortune
on light bulbs.

LETHARGY

Don't disturb my lethargy

my rocking chair time,

don't disturb my musing

my making silly rhyme

don't disturb my silence

my keeping within

don't disturb my dying

my beginning again. . .

LEAVING SUBURBIA

Days are the ticking of the clock
goin' round, alarms sound
beginning the day's race
through green, yellow, red,
green, yellow, red
changing too fast in the day.
slowed down to flashing in the night.
Pedestrians march past city pigeons
seldom startled into flight,
church bells chiming
car alarms beeping and whining
merchants unlocking and raising their gates.
Clank of change in computerized drawers,
retrograde fashions clogging the stores,
clandestine smokers blocking office building doors.
Fast cars with vanity plates
pass panhandlers with box card signs
begging the movers for ten times a dime.

And some dark shady man
sellin' contraband
taps me on the shoulder.
He said, *"We ain't gonna get much older,*
seems all the world is thieves,
straight at the top,
it ain't gonna stop
this foolish land of plenty bit,
and you and I we be getting' by,
by just ignoring all this shit."
He said, *"Take my hand you*
gotta make a stand to deal with
this unnatural life." He said, *"Have*
a smoke, you'll see it's all a joke,
then you'll be naturally aware,
then you won't have to care,
'bout sellin' and buyin'
your soul."

Wind blows suddenly against
a porch chime, angelic sound
slows down too fast time
jangled on the wind.

WARNINGS: LOS ANGELES RIOTS

The fires this time
leveled the cement jungle
and forced open the eyes of the weary
and hardened the hearts of the wary
and sent out a clear and decisive warning
of more days of sitting in mourning
of more children born without a good home
of more boys determined to roam
through snow white streets of plenty.

The fires this time
smoked out the stories of forgotten struggles
while the stagnancy of the powerless
is money to burn
in the fires this time
the kindling is neglected dreams
startled into waking day
by centuries of betrayal.
The fires this time
sent out a clear and decisive warning.

FOR CARLOTTA WHO DIED AT THE AGE OF 20
(a soldier in Angola)

We want our daughters
to be able to dance again,
in firelight and moon glow—
we want them to pass their blood
to fertile ground,
through rite of passage,
rather than under the pressure
shrapnel stopping their hearts.

We do not want to be here,
merely to make the boys laugh,
or the men to lick their lips
and drip obscenities on our breasts.
We do not want to bare down
hard in our bellies to
have infants born into this
loveless gray world.

We want our light
like aurora,
like simmering heat reflected
from shafts of golden grain,
to come not from m-16's and grenades:
but from round tables
filled with fruit and brown bread
and hands
not afraid of holding each other.

We want peace,
because we're tired of giving up
our children to orphanages
and dirt in fields overwhelmed
with the stench of gasoline
burnings of week-old flesh.
We want peace,
because it's been so long
since we could dance unafraid,
and we want so much
for our mother land to heal.

AFRIKANER—PART I
(The Famine)

I want you to remember
when my skin was mahogany,
my nostrils flared and following
the scent and breath of the land,
when my hair rose, kinky and wild,
when I painted my body
with root color,
and gathered fire and spirit
with bared chest.

I want you to remember
when sunrise comes
dusting off dreams
sun circle going round
slow rhythm,
no stress,
in village of kin
when weapons need only
capture wild things,
for roasting flesh to bone
to tools for
skinning cover.

I want you to remember
when river and rain
found their way
to seed from last year's
gleaning left untouched;
and fruit and grain
were able to grow.

I want you to remember
when putting one's back
to the land meant life
and ritual,
when sweat was like honey,
and honey was really manna,
and Africa a promised land of her own.

I want you to remember
when we bore our children
being held by sisters, and mothers
and herb, and heat, and scream,
from one womb,
to Africa's womb,
milk flowed in the breasts
of proud mothers.

I want you to remember
the drum call
the drum call
bare footed stomping
into moon soil,
rite of passage,
holding hands,
chanting we belong,
we belong, with everything here.
The drum, the drum, the drum,
fires, starlight through
tree shadows bright eyes
mahogany faces…

because now
there is no more milk,
in some places,
no more proud mahogany daughters
in others,
and those children left
do not remember, will not wait
to dance to dance like their
elders,
too soon they hear death calling
too soon in the barren night
it comes crawling,
into their withering skins.
Who will remember then?

TOO COOL REFLECTIONS ON THE DOUBLE DIGIT DOUBLE HELIX
(for the year 1988)

I will remember the double digit,
double helix of this year's passing
as an education, a transformation,
of the language I knew as a child.
Where the crack is no longer a line
in the side walk that
you don't want to step on
in case you break
your mother's back
or fall through to China.

Where AIDS is
an unpopular appetite supressant,
that doesn't help anyone,
where the greenhouse effect is no longer,
confined to botanical decorators,
where rap doesn't mean on a door,
and snow isn't Frosty's middle name any more.
The year of the double digit,
double helix, double talk, where
home girl and homeboy-ease have moved
"Val-speak" back to Silicon Valley.

The year that baby boomers grown up
are yuppies, and buppies, and recovering
ex-hippies driving BMWs and Mazdas and Subarus,
and Cherokees, and rebuilt Bugs,
where rolfing is no longer throwing up
after too many beers
and EST is more than just a useful suffix.

The year of the double digit,
double helix, where double faced
preachers, and soldiers, and defenders
of the public faith, aired dirty laundry
like they were in a heat,
and for a long time the flames just kept getting hotter.

The year where neutral planes are
accidently shot down, and double talking
emissaries try to explain the mistakes away,

and double breasted business men, carry
baggage and bombs, labeled with the invisible
words retaliation, revenge, and martyr over
Lockerbie,
just three days before Christmas.

The year of the double digit, double helix,
where just saying no is in, tobacco is out,
being straight is cool and getting too buzzed
isn't hot anymore. Except it's been the year
where blood isn't just a brother, but red
scarffed crack runner with nothing but a bunch
of bad rap and a cloud to wrap 'round you
to keep you coming back.

Coming back to the year of the double digit,
double helix, on the downside where,
water is no longer taken for granted,
and trees are being counted like
the hairs on a balding head. The
year where the spotted animals are preserved
like the nails on a fine hand.
The year where, the new age baby boomer
recovering ex-hippies write their own language,
make their own kind of music, while teenagers
turn into skin heads, and wait in the wings,
with a language of their own.

The language doesn't stop changing,
just keeps on coming harder and harder,
on the helix on the loop
the baby boomer's babies
prefer granola to Wonder Bread,
Adidas to Keds,
Nintendo to Monopoly,
there is no end to the loop,
on the helix,
there is no end to this loop.

THE PEACE POEM

Peace comes
in the middle of the night
dark no sound
no horns
no children crying,
no clack of high heals,
no TV all night news,

No arguments,
no accusations,
no assumptions.

Listen. . .
there is the wind
        in the trees,
listen…
there is indeed room
for peace.

ON BECOMING AN ARTIST

You learn how
to hide your true face,
from this person
perhaps just show the
flicker of recognition
to another
but never too much of
the eyes
you learn to keep
almost everyone on
the periphery of
your inner circle
so you won't have to care
too much—you're not callous
just not wanting to get too
involved in a thing
that doesn't bring out
your passion—
you push things around
in your rooms, while
sorting out things on your mind
you take long trips alone
and sink further and further
into the only thing that has
ever made any sense
to you, and you wonder
if this is what it's like to be
an addict—the not caring
if anyone else in the world
knows that you're alive—
you finally understand the
whole thing a little clearer
and realize that with them
there, you can't, don't, won't,
fall deeper and deeper into the
only place that you can
depend on—and slowly
you metamorphose
between two worlds

knowing that still they don't,
won't, can't let you come here
to work alone for too long,
they demand
to see one of your faces
to make you over in
their own image and
you become good at
giving them
what they want
though you wished they knew
that you were always hungry
for what they couldn't give back.

NOSEY LADY LAMENT

This poem is ignoring the mail,

it won't let me get up to

answer the phone or the knock

of the door to door magazine

hustler who's working on a

scholarship to college.

This poem makes me tired

but procrastination's bubble

is bursting—patterns are

forming—recollection of

words looking for a life line

move through my

mind like a warning—this poem

has just about given up

waiting for me to pay attention

this poem is moving on. . .

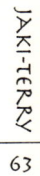

JAKI-TERRY

III. DESTRUCTION CYCLE:
DRIVE BY SHOOTINGS

"If you believe in love
And all that love can bring
A brand new day
A brand new way
Will you make a case for it
If you will, then come along with me..."

"Come Along With Me" by Gimbel and Sample from
The Song Lives On CD featuring Lalah Hathaway.

TO UNDERSTAND IS TO UNDERSTAND
(a day in the life of a Diva)

i need to understand
why you keep injectin' yourself in the middle of my self-definition,
my self actualization.
how did you come to the conclusion
that this was or it is about for or against you? am i to understand that
the only thing you see is rebellion when you gaze upon my notty dreds?
would we even be havin' this conversation if i were white?

you need to understand
this ain't about you, your anger, your fears
or your political-correctness (whatever that means)
i stand proud in my temple, in my woman-ness, in the skin i'm in
and every pore of my being celebrates life in all of its simplicity
now i need to understand: are you angry, or just afraid?

afraid to live and let live, afraid to let yourself give
permission to the person in the mirror to step out on faith? cuz i need to
understand
why you look the other way when i face you like a sista with no fear?
why you whisper behind my back while i move through this life in peace?
what it is about my nappy head that causes a commotion in your solar plexus?
that disrupts your
central nervous system? that angsts you to the nth degree? Is this about you or
me?

you need to understand
this is the way Creation made me—the beauty in all things is what you need to
see
since we're on the subject, you need to be aware
there's a soul & spirit under my notty hair
beauty is what beauty does, understand that from the start
besides, God ain't judgin hair, God judgin' hearts!

PERCEPTIONS

perceptions hiding under the guise of knowing
are really a showing a prejudice
& I guess y'all don't understand that
perceptions necessarily got nothin' to do with
truth

perceptions hiding under the cloak of summation
is really a perpetuation
of the very dysfunction you say you want to resolve
tell me, how are you livin?
are you about forgivin'
or forever givin' grief where there jus' oughta be
a lil' more love?

perceptions masqueradin' as discernment
are really a deterrent for a real healing
& I got a feeling that until we move past
perception, that lethal injection
wheels will forever spin & the world will forever be in
turmoil with no hope for tomorrow

perception
costed 1 billion people their lives on their way to amerikkka
perception
costed millions their lives on the way to the gas chamber
perception costed millions their lives in the name of civilization
& when will we stop this mess, when the rest of us are gone, too?

perception, what a bullshit word for assumption
when will we ever get the gumption
to move past the stench of perception
that deadly infection
& just deal with one another in peace?

I WANNA TELL MY BABIES
(for Chris)

i wanna tell my babies 'bout
rosa parks
i wanna tell my babies 'bout fannie lou
i wanna give my chil'ren the method & message
so they can make herstory
come true

i wanna tell my babies 'bout
paul laurence dunbar
marcus garvey, too
i wanna give my chil'ren songs in the key of life
like stevie wonder do

i want dey dreams ta be
in six-part sweet honey rockin' harmony
& see the beauty of the world
in their own eyes
through the mirrors of mine

i wanna tell my babies
the whole story
the one they wouldn't let my ancestors tell

i want my babies to know the truth!

UNTITLED #1002

i move through this life
with child-like faith
& a machete between my teeth
cuttin' through these critical times,
hard to deal with

i manipulate like a ninja
through the madness of
it's gonna get a whole lot worse
before it gets a whole lot better

i move through this life
with eyes on the prize
& pray incessantly
for the other side of the
rainbow!

CONDITIONS

i'll love you on the condition that you love yourself
otherwise, you can't love me
i'll love you on the condition that you be yourself
& and let me be me
to love yourself & be yourself is only human, you see?
there's no other way to give your love unconditionally!

i'll love you on the condition that you give me room to grow
to let me learn about myself & let my spirit glow
love me on the condition that i will do the same
so we both have something to share and receive
without guilt or blame

 i'll love you on the condition that you make no conditions on me
love makes it own conditions
unconditionally
i only ask to receive from what you want from me
let love be the Master / only love holds the key
be fair with me & share with me
i'm more than your lover, i'm your best friend
i'm on your side, love is my guide
from point begin to end!

IN SEARCH OF RAINBOWS
(For J.J.)

sometimes, in searching for our rainbows
we find ourselves face to face
with our demons/ not knowing how to fight back
too scared / stubborn to roll over & die
so we still try
feebly, but an effort, nonetheless

sometimes you gotta hit your bottom to jump at the sun
make your refuge with Infinite Power
so that nothing is against you
make the connection
cuz you haven't forgotten how to pray

when we join hands with that power
we find we have the power to put our demons behind us
we discover that our own best friend
is the person in the mirror
& the rainbow is tied around our hearts!

BEFORE WE HEAL
(for J.J.)

we lie, deny, justify
all the reason why we opt to destroy the person we call
me, myself, i
as we drag our tattered psyches around
like death waiting for our funerals
we attempt to put on a noble front to the world
& those we love that "i'm o.k."

we lie, deny, justify
because its easier & safer than confrontation
it's less strain than bearing the burden
of being responsible, for taking charge of this life
called ones' own; chaos becomes chaotic, but because

we lie, deny, justify
we convince ourselves this is easier to live with
than questioning our worth; this is easier to live with
than making the commitment to do something different
admitting defeat is easier than
admitting that with
positive power, a positive life is indeed ours to have

                                        for the taking…have it
                                        for the asking… have it…
                                        for the believing… have it…
                                        for the achieving… have it …
                                              so… because

we lie, deny, justify
once again satan is the victor
& another angel in heaven cries

we lie, deny, justify
because something in us feels unworthy, unwilling
to raise our eyes to the sky & home seems like such a far-away place,
such a foreign place

no, this conversation isn't over when we cross the threshold
no, this conversation isn't over when we close our eyes
no, this conversation isn't over when we go about our way, cuz
when we go on
lying, denying, justifying
once again, satan wins
& another angel cries
one more angel dries his eyes

TRUTH DON'T NEED A NAME

you felt it from
the beginning
but you're afraid that
if you give it a name
it might fly away or worse, yet
you might wake up
& find its all your mind's
illusion

well, dream it isn't
& wings it hasn't
& even if it could fly
where would it go but
back to its source
to be sent out, yet again?

what it is
is what it is
& what's more
it's very real
whether you choose to
name it or not
if it had wings
it would wrap you in them

& if it were a dream
it would kiss your eyes
in the morning
to face the reality
that's before you

LEO SUN, SCORPIO MOON, CANCER...RISING – I

I.
i write pretty poems
to keep my scorpio in check
otherwise, I just might start a riot
or wreck shit on purpose all to pieces
& laugh my ass off
while I'm doin' the fire walk
'round bloody, heaving bodies
in my full-moon ritual
(it's a woman thang, ya'll)

i write pretty poems
cuz my cancer stills the waters
risin' to the top of my
      don't rock my groove scorpio I'm painin'
      but i'll never show you the dark side
the one you wished you had time to hide from
if somebody only warned you sooner

i write pretty poems
cuz my leo sun loves me & protects she from
      scorpio moon might sting myself
      call on cancer mama moon risin'
      rock me gently into the night
it's gonna be alright, yebo, it's gonna be alright

i write pretty poems
to appease the beast manifestin' as medusa
      turn you into stone jus' as sure as to look at your ass
if scorpio moon gets wind that you treated her sistas foul

i write pretty poems
with leonine grace & call on cancer mama moon risin
      hush little baby, don't say a word
to save my chil'un...

II.
i write pretty poems
cuz therapy is expensive
i figure with a pen in my hand
& a poem in my heart
the Lord & me can work this out ourselves

MIAMI BEACH

I. Yemoja

i fell in love with her
the first time i smelled her essence in the balmy breeze
i trembled with awe as she swayed her majestic blue body
from beach to infinity before my eyes
my offerings of fruit, molasses, my favorite bracelet, my tears
all seemed minute in her expanse of turquoise
so i prostrated myself before her majesty

she washed her shells, coral & sand around my swollen ankles
she kissed me full in the mouth with her waves
she received my prayers with opened arms
& baptized me in the bosom of her love
> "rest your worries on my broad shoulders,
> experience your rebirth in my womb of amniotic mother-love
> sleep in my arms under bright stars & crescent moon
> & i'll sing you my lullaby of ages
> commune with creation & i will send your request to the clouds

& bless
> your head with sweet rain!   welcome to my
> house: remove your sandals, daughter, you're standing on
> sacred ground!"

grandmother of forevers, i receive you with outstreched arms
my heart & cup overflows
& i love you doesn't capture it all

bless you mama, may we share eternity together
i look to return to you again...

II. Two Sisters Praying

two sisters praying under a starry sky
flying on the wings of sistership
with comrades far away
two sisters communing with mother earth & father time
leaning on the shoulders of yemoja
& a star falls

III. The Dolphin Dances

it's like an addiction
calling me out of sound sleep
beckoning me to sit at her side
& talk to her
i need to be here to find answers
to find solace
to just be one with the Creator
& the sea children watch
i pray
with outstretched arms
on knees bended
with heart extended
pleading my request to the universe
to lay my burden down, & i lay it down
at yemoja's feet

a star falls
& a dolphin dances

IV. Back Home

spirit said,
    "move your bed off the wall, point your head north!
    to the east is where Creation lives—pray to the east!
    to the west is where is where the day goes—leave your past behind!
    to the south is where your work lives—move your feet
    the north is where your dreams live & your answers to all your questions—
        listen!"

i sleep
& astral travel back to the place where i first met her
she calls me to her to come sit for a spell
i am once again, spellbound

i walk through the waves naked & calm
5 dolphins move towards me & ride me out to the sea on their backs
they circle around my head to watch over me
while i sleep fetal at the bottom of the ocean
yemoja rocks me with her rhythm

i can breathe under the salty sea

i am peaceful
i am home

i awaken
to the light of the candles burning in my apartment
but it was no dream, i know i was there
i'm wiping salt water from my eyes
& removing sand from my teeth

1994
(reflections on my 38th year)

this is my year for learning gratitude
this is my year for learning to love life

i've watched another move on to other places
i've learned to love smiles on human faces

i've sat at yemoja's feet & cried my spirit into her
while she sang eibe eiye in my ear & rained blessing

after blessing into my soul
i've slept fetal in her belly & remembered

the first sound i ever heard in the universe
was my mother's voice vibrating through my body

yet unborn
i've learned to walk like a samurai on purpose

just like her
& in finding my own power, found humility

by pressing my face against the expanse of sky & sea
i've learned that goodness comes forth when you pray for it
& that even in hard times, there's a lesson in everything

i've learned how to lean on everlasting arms
& learned not be anxious by sitting at the feet of sparrows
while reminding i & i to take long deep meaningful breaths

of this stuff called life
i've learned to thank my Jah in new ways

whenever He paints the sunrise in my favorite shade of pink
i've learned that humor is therapy

so i laugh when i hear the noise of children
& cherish the little girl in me who knows

this day, she gave me her best
i've learned that pray incessantly means just that
& to give thanks always means always having abundance
i've learned that love is everything

especially when He paints the sunset
in my favorite shade of pink

SONG #222

this day, as i self-examine & exorcise all demons
bathe myself from every defilement of the flesh
'stay clean & be ready'   i feel fire in my feet

the quiet in my ears as i move
heart to the mind to the Most High
incessantly   reverently   always

& lovingly joyously peacefully patiently kindly
faithfully, mercifully sharpened Divinely
as i submit to whom i owe it all

i suit up for battle slowly & steady
getting ready to stand firm
& watch the miracle happen before my eyes!

POINSETTIAS

in my windowsill in june
reminding me of your december smiles
& prayer becomes a ritual thing all the time
when i recline in thoughts of you

the essence of a conjure shared by a best friend
home from her journey wafts through my brain
the melon & the mood are ambrosia as we
bask in the glow of each other's light

i can feel my mother's love all around me
this dawn day; i awaken to the truth that the miracle
is not in the manifestation, but the power of the Divine
& thank you, while inadequate, are the only words i can utter

on my roof overlooking downtown in the late heat of
a late spring / preview to a summer kinda groove
the light reflects through the stained glass, just so
cinnamon dances with white rose from tunisia,

lavender & ylang-ylang weaves its magic around my heart
in & out of rooms that i go to for sanctuary & solace,
in places deeper than thought
i take a deep breath,
gaze through the poinsettias in my window in june that are
decorated with your december smiles. . .
& thank you, while inadequate,
are the only words that come to mind

CONVERSATION

they played, they talked
yet, they never exchanged a word
between the hisses & moans wafting
in, out & between a mikki howard croon
all that was never said,
was said that night as they savored over each
other's tongues like a double shot of louis tres,

ever so careful not to spill a drop
they lingered for days
inhaling & exhaling each other's essences
miles of skin stretched out,
heat sensitive & glistening in candlelight
ached to be caressed, kissed, licked & finger stroked
with the deftness of baby's breath & in the quaking of two

spirits in the moment, they ignite each other inside out
& oh, how they loved
all that was heard were the screams & sighs by the light of a crescent
moon softly in each other's ears, echoing through their
eyes all that needed to be said
they embraced each other in

sweat & afterglow
& in memory of the magic they made, every now & again,
they'd glance at each other & smile
as they remembered the day a man & woman made peace, not war
committed each other to a random act of kindness in the moment of

now—just because the universe stopped, for a blink,
so twin flames could affirm & move forward to the rhythm
of the ancestor's drum

PEACOCK
(for Eric)

coral, eucalyptus, a basket full of notes
tied with fuchsia ribbon, a fine bone
china cup etched in gold trim for
serving orange juice to oshun nestles
next to a siamese cat filled with moonglow.

next to the champa sticks, in between the
pale blue candles whose wick needs a
trim, stands two empty candle holders,
her small bible & five dimes that
frame the right side of his face. he

rests his head against a black lacquer
jewel box with peacocks carved
in mother-of-pearl. while the unicorn
pauses overhead to watch, the
parrot stands on his left shoulder,

poised. five dimes & a basket of
herbs move along the mantle in a
sea of blue, mauve & white. a brass
horn to remember music; five brass
candle holders to remember prayer.

a bouquet of carnations, mums, daisies
sprayed with baby's breath is the
offering of thanksgiving that she
brings, placing the small vase
between the rose of jericho & coral

to his left. he's dressed in blue
& posed pensively. she lights incense
while saying a prayer for him & places
in his left hand, a stone that was
washed so smooth, a heart was hollowed

out. she remembers finding it while
they were beach combing in midsummer.
beneath his feet, oshun watches
beneath her skirt, five open jugs of
water for libations & dreams. the

ashes in the smudge pot cool while she
gazes at the yellow candle burning
brightly beneath him. he returns
the stare, eyes posed pensive—
& oshun watches, laughing . . .

ABSTRACT
(for Ron)

she loves afrikan dolls, songbirds made
of porcelain, small statues carved
in mahogany wood & soapstone, three-
year old zinfandel, sweet incense to
mingle with her conversations

to the Almighty; she loves him
like eternity sitting on his right
shoulder. job's tear reminds her to
be patient with him always.
the man with the child in his eyes

requests eternal playtime & so the
plan is laid out. this is her own
quiet place; to ask Spirit to walk
with him; to make the abstract
plain, to make chaos sane

to find paradise in the moment of now.
obatala, the wise one, the sage,
is watching over this one. the
drum sits close by as the abstract
& the actual

join forces to guide him.
& when she stands closely, he sends
the drum through her feet, making her
dance the dance of her grandmother's
grandmother; & when she dances,

he exhales a wall of fire around her
that her dance may be purified; &
when her garments are as white
as snow, he opens her heart
like a lotus blossom

& when her heart is open as wide
as the sky, he jumps in head long
to be resurrected, renewed, healed.
he jumps in to die & be reborn
die & be reborn...

& obatala hears his prayers...

HIS EYES TALK...
(to beautiful black men everywhere)

because he lives in me in a very ancient place
& as he gazes through my soul, by the way of my third eye
i am charged to remember now who i was then

his eyes talk in whispers bearing gifts
gifts bearing fruit on the vine: harvest, kwanzaa
ritual, prayer sanctuary   his eyes talk hope, preservation

protection   because he is me in a very real way
i see myself looking through his mirror
& we both radiate in each other's excellence

his eyes talk as he remembers being in the presence
of the present; because he really loves that kind of special
his eyes talk love always...

& my eyes are always close by, always listening

7 YEARS LATER...

with Jehovah guardin my back
in the name of Christ Jesus
        ache'   ache'   ache'

with angels
        all night   all day watchin ovah me
           my Lawd

& mama's voice whispering in my ear
    "sounds like recovery to me"
everyday   before i fall on my knees to pray...

can't nothin hurt me
can't nothin harm me
i'm invincible!

A GHETTO GIRL'S LOVE SONG

it's something about the way you loved my skin with finger strokes so soft, that made me want to
get to know you, up close & personal the first time i saw you
something about those eyes; ever so engaging, drank me in, told me the truth
& not just what I wanted to hear, so i listen
i listen, i learn, i love you

believe it, this ain't even about sex

it's about the way you loved my heart with finger strokes so soft, that made me want to
get to know you up close & personal the first time i saw you
something about your presence; commanding, self-assured, stoic, regal in the midst of
milleniums of madness—made me feel safe
& gave me space to be me, so i listen,
i listen, i learn, i love you

then again, maybe this is about sex

it's just because it's something about the way you loved my mind with finger strokes so, so soft
that made me want to get to know you up close & personal the first time i saw you
something about the words you spoke; so honest & bare to the bone—made me know
you, too, have walked through fire; yet your clothes are not singed, so listen ,
i listen, i learn, i love you

believe it, then again, let me show you!

ODE TO WEEQUAIC HEIGHTS
(just another day ...for Queen Latifah)

i'll always miss summer days of chess & backgammon
acey-deucey; run it back; lemonade & 'RVR
& the first time i heard my sweet sista minnie sing a song of life on my sunporch
a game in progress; 21; run it back; *"yo, i got next up!"* straight off the 107—
south orange
after a long day of bitin' the apple

      just another day up in the 'hood
      another day around the way

i'll forever miss the winter nights of spades & uno on the big red table in my livin' room
"draw four—green! ha-ha!;" "run it back"; vibin' with sista friends on a "lets-get-together" tip
earl pluckin' my heartstrings on the stereo & al jarreau singin' 'alonzo' all around my heart while shekere & drums call angie back home to a dream via WBLS
droste, amaretto with cognac and kalua with cream was the nectar of queens in apt. b-4

      just another day up in the 'hood
      another day around the way

& how about those weeks of cartoons & cold, sweet cereal
tickles & hugs with my jenaiel & kia; run it back; kool-aid & 101.9 & nights of me and kyle sharin' secrets in quiet whispers over burgers, fries & friday night videos; run it back; 107 back to the apple monday mornin' with your walkman in your ear while ziggy & the chil'ren give you, your dose & soul II soul keeps you on your path back to life—back to reality; run it back

      just another day up in the hood
      another day around the way

SOMETIME'S IT AIN'T ALL ABOUT SEX

sometimes i wanna jus' fit next to you in bed
in that little spot you've created jus' for me
& feel your soft breath on the back of my neck
while we sleep

sometimes i jus' wanna hold that glance in my head
in the moment
for all time cuz i'm needy like dat
& i don't alla time feel the need
to explain the thousands of ways you warm my toes
on cold nights
& make me laugh with no effort
& soothe me with sounds that music's like lullabies

sometimes i wanna jus' hold your vision in my eyes
wid both hands
cuz we both daydream in the same key
& trip the light fantastic like stardust on an
august night

then there are times when i jus' wanna stand serene
in our space of endless commune
in our silence of always knowin'
that sometimes, we say much
without words

sometimes i jus' wanna know that you know…

THEN THERE ARE TIMES...

when a sista's gotta raise a lil' sand
every now & again
cuz pain & logic ain't got no business in the same room
let alone the same sentence
i mean there are jus' them days when you decide
it ain't vogue to be an amazon
& you jus' can't find a broom & dustpan big enuf
to sweep up your sanity
& your self-esteem, too

what's a girl to do?

there are jus' those times
ya know, them times
that mama didn't warn you about
like—ultra brite toothpaste
& lovers who need more than you're able to give
this votin' day
& lonely nights when the walls talk
& not being able to say good-bye
even though one day
we all gotta go
& whats up wid dis AIDS shit
any damn way?!?

on days like these
rationale can kiss my ass
i need to wail like bessie
wid three fingas of remy
& someone who will listen
jus' listen!

PSALMS 139:14
(make ya clap ta dis! All Praises!!)

in a fear-inspiring way
i am bad!
You, who knew me when
i was my mama's secret secret
knew secretly that one day
i would write this poem of praise

in a fear-inspiring way
i am wonderfully made!
a sho' nuff for real in the flesh no joke
You, who knew my realities
while they were still my dreams
who knew even the embryo of me
all praises, all praises
to You!

in a fear-inspiring way
Your lessons are only a miracle,
the greatest being,
allowing me one more day
one more way
to show your love
through me!

Chezia Thompson Cager

IV. Rejuvenation Cycle:
Taking It to the Streets

"...No life can escape being blown about
by the winds of change and chance.
And though you may never know
all the steps
you must learn to join the dance..."

"Through Heaven's Eyes" by Stephen Schwartz
The Prince of Egypt CD soundtrack

UNDER FLOWER: THE 1983 MARCH ON WASHINGTON

        leopardess
        howling under a full moon
        as a quarter million souls
        or more
        ascend the hive cone
my blood arrives
        in Torrents
        using **all mediums to move**
        all voices to sing
        all rhythms to March
my blood flows . . . Outward
        to the giant Black Glassmaker
        with one eye
        He is translucent yet solid
        Ages Old
        Vibrating in Eight / Perfect in Seven
        My twin in the Number Two
        "The Winds and the waves
        shall obey my will—Peace Be Still!"
        Two centuries later
        we are still warring
            for what **"The Word" gave us**
        Twenty years later
        Darkie Nightsongs are still
        the only weapons we have
        against **"The JACKAL"**
        "Let My People Go—Let them go?"
falling, my blood rains
        So that savage—dancing in White
        I Jump Rope on The Axis
        Not Chanting "WE SHALL OVERCOME . . ."
        but singing **"This li'l light of mine**
Oh, I'm gonna let it,   **gonna let it shine"**
I'm not a Rainbow under this Sun
but I AM A Slowly Dissolving BLUE Song
in Ogotemeli's* mouth
at Dusk—Hear ME?
Oh,
   Say
      Can
         You
           See?

*Master Dogon Philosopher interviewed in *Conversations with Ogotemeli*.

LA FLEUR HAITIENNE
(for Dr. Diane Sandaker)

sun blotched iris
lines in Venetian eyes
lost in future lines
going nowhere
going everywhere
at once—this woman spirit
divided
one-into-one-into-one
the pentatonic heartbeat
generating infinite curves
infinite lines—her beauty
is confused by generations of miscegenation
in extremism

> **be** a two-timed divorced wife
> **be** a traditional grandmother in a
> contemporary culture
> **be** a discontented mother
> **play pretend a white girl**
> **play pretend a creole lady**

She is cake-walk beauty
like sugar and butter melted
rum beauty—golden and intoxicating
shallow shoulder—twisted strides
fine mind
She will make a good soldier

> **Grimace, "I cannot understand them!"**
> and she cannot
> tiny hands with eaten nails
> woman's body—woman's desire
> curious careful eyes
> the calm detached pose
> of lava rising at eighteen
> tense caramel-colored form erupting
> like the **Dance of a Volcano**

FORBIDDEN FRUIT

transgressing the lines
of forbidden behavior
I sic paralysis on
a society of normalization

by writing
I pass us through
"determinate historical content"
and experience us today

long winded sighs
chagrinned helloes
the pursuit of different lifestyles
predictable provocations
in attempted heterotopias

it is an old story
that bites red
like apple skins
taste bitter like kola
slides smooth like banana
and is cool to the alien touch

MLK

sequencing **Time**
The Nothing finds us
Something and we whisper
"Why We Can't Wait..."
logic's dissolution says
there is something
to find and tell
Something told to spark the
discourses of madness
medicine, punishment
and sexuality fearlessly
"Why Can't WE Wait?"
as the seconds chase
you into a corner
and you bare your breast
like a man
waiting for **Time**
to stop

LA DANSE DU DRAGON
(Pour Dragon avec amour)

> **"Drag on wind in a corna**
> **N' I start twistin' me body here**
> **N' when we meet in de centa. . ."**
>
> from **"Dragon Dance"**
> by the **Mighty Sparrow**

She waits
as one thin ring of **Blue** Water
circling to house the spectrum of **Orange**
folding into that **Forest Brown** and shadowed
Blue-Black iris jazz.

    He cannot cross water!

Oshun knows that watching him
turning and twisting on her boundaries
STANDING
to stretch against **GOD**
as the Archmage reminds us,

"Dragons are older and wiser than men
and that He is kin to Orm Embar and Kalessin*
like them limb from limb."

Dark nipples rippling over hued muscles
a sculptured face
        a chiseled portrait of Power
            a half-century old,
grown in the **mahogany** and **red**
painted by a Calypsonian
and tempered by a Steel Pan.

Sounding a boy's fragility
housed in a man's body
struggling with
the walking, restless sleep
of a Child dreaming on a beach
            in Trinidad
      A Child who wakes to Oppression
and speaks war
with a gesture:

    "Make no peace with slavery
    Make no peace for you have survived. . ."**

Here a full moon grows a picture
as it tries to match
the lucid choreography of a Giant Talking
to the thunder in **Shango's** hand

Giant Talking to the Flowers:

Hand under Earth,
She under flower

**Remembering the common denominator of man
is not power but knowing .   .   .
divining one is.   .   .
that we should be.   .   .**
Moving in GOD's space
masked only by Time
and the scales of a Baptist preacher's
White clothes

Swaying and roaring in that

melodic,
       hallelujah
              trill

the Laughter that can Kill

        **The Dragon STANDS
        Makes a Fearsome Face
        Lifts his Wings
        And breathes FIIIRRRE**

So that hypnotized
The Water is consumed
purified and made anew
in the Carnival **Blue**
of a forest God's archipelago
        of unknown dimensions.

  *Dragons in Ursula Le Guin's *Earth Sea Trilogy*.
**Words spoken by the character Aldrick in
  The Dragon Can't Dance by Earl Lovelace.

A BLACK HISTORY MONTH POEM
*(for Buckwheat, the Governor of Virgina's Cat,
and all Confederate License Plate holders)*

Emasculation
as the **ART** of the **DEAL: A**
broader hand with Lincoln's
five separate but equal fingers:
Distinct as life forms
inhabiting different planets.
Invisible woMan in a
protected union:
A new kind of enslavement.
*"Oh, I wish I was in the
Land of Cotton
Ole Times there are not
Forgotten
Look Away, Look A-Way
Look Away Dixieland..."*
Emasculation
as the punch line in the
Code Noire, Jim Crow and
Separate but equal statutes
that make me less than human
on sight in the latter 20th century;
As Dubois' color line prevails
as the appropriate cultural
context to ascertain political status
and social disposition
and availability for a lynch dragging
in Texas, here, there and everywhere
where there is zero level of
comfort with an unassimilated Negro.
And I know my will
my daily effort to
push skyward as
a creative being
requires a vigilant
hierarchical
power to be kept in
check, because
    driving on t*he Freeway*
        of love
with a whuus, a flake and
an ego maniac can be
dangerous to your health.

HOUSE MADE OF DAWN*
(for my Daddy, The Arkansas Timber Wolf)

house of evening
light singing my
      body
Wa-I ha Wa-I haha
dance of the light
stream riding purple
ponies in clear flowing
strides: ancestor voice
urges, *"you must run—*
those who run are
the life that flows in our
      people"
Daughter of Blackfeet
Clan, howling in Arkansas
Timber Wolf Time, with
Father getting drunk for the last
Time, playing ragtime piano under
a red moon as an act of beauty,
      dancing
in pin-stripped elegance
  feathers in hand
Wa-I ha Wa-I haha
spinning webs of light
in the Fancy Dance
of the Street's Dawn

*Novel title by N. Scott Momaday

I THOUGHT HE WAS A PLANT

night shadows play havoc
on the sky covering dusk
like a giant swaying tree
you tower over me
I always thought
I was tall for a girl
but you engulf me
like a taller version of myself
with sides burns
lean—like me
with angles and lines
that fit my curves
like a giant swaying tree
you sink your roots into
the Earth
and she moans
cause she can remember
what's coming
…"*And submission is easy baby*
I always knew it would be".*
like the wind around
a giant swaying tree
I sing Isis' ancient songs of spring
    cause you are a plant
    and I am the dew
    under a moon struck night.

* line from an Aretha Franklin song

CHANSON D'AMOUR CREOLE
(pour Haiti)

(Très bien merci
Pierre Andre Muzac
Arthur Francois &
Rudolphe Prudent
for your assistance with the
Francais & Creole translations.)

parfois
quand le diamant
dans votre oeil
attrappe le soleil
et courtise ainsi
le feu, cel fait brûler
l'amour à l'intèrieur

je suis endièrement brûlé
dans ce coucher de soleil
c'est l'été
et la maturité de la
brise
est infectueuse
Nous rion toi, moi
et les fleurs poussent
embaumées et chaudes
de vie

la terre est comme nous
noire et douce
La Meringue est une
sauvagette dans mon souffle

Tu es un grand homme
et brun
Je suis la plume
à tourner
à glisser
à balayer
à travers le rhythme
le terre nous invite
et our répondons
avec la musique
de nos mains

CREOLE LOVE SONG
(for Haiti)

(Thank you very much
Pierre Andre Muzac
Arthur Francois &
Rudolphe Prudent
for your assistance with the
French & Creole translations.)

there are times
when the diamond
in your eyes
catches the sun
and so sparks
the fire within
that allows love to burn

I am aglow
in this sunset
it is summer
and the ripeness
of the air
is infectious
We smile you and I
and the flowers bloom
fragrant and warm
with life

the earth is like us
black and sweet
The Meringue is a
wildness in my breathing

You are tall man
and brown
I am the feather
to turn
to slide
to sweep
across the rhythm
the earth invites us
and we answer
with the music
of our hands

Je ne suis pas fatigué chéri	I'm not tired baby
Je transpire seulement	I'm jus running wet
Je ne suis pas fatigué chéri	I'm not tired baby
Je transpire seulement	I'm jus running wet
Tu peux essayer chéri	You can try baby
nais tu ne peux pasm 'arrêter	but you can't stop me yet
Dis je suis fatigué	Say I'm tired of the way
de la mauvaise façon dont tu	you treat me so mean
me traites	
Mon nouvel homme	My new man's comin
vient dans la cammionnette	on the Camionette
Pauline	Pauline
Il pleut chéri	The rain is fallin baby
Il pleut sur moi	fallin down on me
Il pleut chéri	The rain is fallin baby
Il pleut sur moi	fallin down on me
Si tu viens ici chéri	If you come here honey
Je vais te bercer pour dormir	I'm gonna rock you to sleep
Le coumbite sonne	The coumbites ringin
sonne dans toute la ville	ringin all over town
Le coumbite sonne	The coumbites ringin
sonne dan toute la ville	ringing all over town
Balancer cette machette	Swinging that machete
tuera un gentilhomme	will break a good man down
Un jour, chéri	Someday baby
seuls toi et moi, oui	jus you and me, yes
un jour chéri	Someday baby
seuls toi et moi	jus you and me
partirons	We're gonna ride away
au ciel	to heaven
dans la camionette	in the camionnette
Pauline	Pauline
L'enfant est comme toi	The child is like you
eveillé et curieux	vibrant and searching

Comme toi il trouve
mon sein
chaud et récomfortant
Je donnerais
tout ce que je possède
et même plus
pour la joie
que tu m'as apportée
cher mari de mon corps et
de mon âme
père de mon Enfant
feu de mon Coeur

Like you he finds
my breast
warm and comforting
I would give
all that I have
and much more
for the happiness
you have brought me
Husband of my being

Father of my Child
Fire of my Heart

A DATE WITH DESTINY
*(with thanks to Keith Glover
for* "Thunder Knocking At My Door"*)*

Thunder
is like the
shivering of
night owls
in dense forest darkness
catastrophically ruffled
and showered in light
with the music of lithe
motion to quicken the
pulse to dance the ancient
tongues of Erzulie's meetings
in Congo Square.

Thunder
is a spirit
not wholly
holy born
out of the energy
which is music laden
with his morality calling
out to me in diamond impulses
because here, I lay
under a blossoming Plum Tree
as fire in God's magnifying glass
glowing.

ALIEN PUSSY

"He gives me fever when he kisses
Fever when he holds me tight
Fever in the morning and
*Fever all through the night"**

kidnapped and
genetically enhanced by
black star power
integrated
with no thought
of limitations
Watusi tall
without spike heels
She sashayed into the room
and stopped traffic
and conversation
with her Fischer body
(her Intel mind was her secret weapon)
the *Meow"*
scared them but they
figured she was just playing
He thought, *"Maybe I'm Not*
too strange for her after all"
and tipped his gambler's hat over
his left eye
She saw his mouth first
the curvaceousness of line and the mole
that suggested he could kiss
and lick her clean on a sunny day
and her whiskers shivered
slightly
swishing that tail of hers
across the floor She danced
a Kat-sho-dou Kata
dropped on all fours
hunched her back and hisssssssed
the women ran out of the room
He thought
"Maybe I got what she needs after all,"
backed into a dark corner and waited
She saw his eyes in the dark
and in her segmented sequential vision

The Moon was already rising
past her planetary door
She had to get him to the ship
"Meow" she said softly
moving toward him
"I don't speak French," He said
leaning against the wall
She began climbing up his body
taking his pulse as she went
purring and smelling
purring and touching
till He grabbed her hands gently
looked deeply into her eyes and
said, *"I think I could like you
but this is a little fast for me
and I'm not sure I know what
to do with alien pussy."*

*song "Fever" by John Davenport, Eddie J. Cooley
on "The Song Lives On" CD by Joe Sample featuring
Lala Hathaway.

JFK, JR.'S LAST FLIGHT

                Tessering*
              through
            womb spaces
          where
        intersecting
      lines form
    crossed kisses
in a flight
horizon of
sunburst spotted
with an
unknown if dark
veil
he finds the courage
to soar.

*A concept of time travel created by novelist Madeline L'Engle.

LA FEMME DU DRAGON: A CHOREOPOEM
(for Barbara Diehl)

My mother's green savannas
are not my bleak steppes
contiguous with canyon faults
razor sharp crags
surrealistic fissures
and liturgical butts,
where I dance in the hollow basin
of shallow tide pools
of Yemanya's blood.
Arbor-borne in the swell of a dream of a
tropical isthmus, I face the bluff of
my shadow— "Come and get me,"
it teases: "Don't you remember?"
The grotto of my initiation
the bog I learned to walk upright within
buttresses my footsteps through the floe
of bad blood, no values
media shock,
racism in the latter 20th century.
The terrorist maelstrom carries me
beyond the range of academic testosterone
over the Cataract of Fatalism
through the Gorge of Machiavelli's meeting to
the Gulch of Judas and
the rise of Joseph from the grave
through the memory of a grove
that contained a burning bush of truth,
leading to Oshun's estuary of life.
My shadow sat down in an abandoned Ford.
I like Mustangs—fast cars.
The shoal was in view of the Mississippi levee,
where I had levitated.
The eddy between had begun to take form
as the Goliath stood up in the mid-air scrub.
An aerial chute left him at
the foothills, within my reach:
and I found myself finally understanding
That ignorance is a cultural legacy
destined for genetic transmission and
that there was nothing left to do
but don my priestess' robes
cross the sandspit
and sacrifice him.

THE DAUGHTER CHRONICLES: THINGS HER BAD BUTT DID

Ludicrous in FUBU Jeans, She
preens in a queenly manner
before any mirror
that stops her beauty

I found my broken china plate,
a rotting half-eaten apple, a container
of orange juice and my red bra
under her bed.

*"Why can't I wear your black
and red underwear?
We wear the same size:
so what's the big deal anyway?
and I think. . ." She goes on.*

Miss Thang is the century's next bomb
if she can slow down long enough to
keep from blowing up
in a designer purple stripped bikini
swimsuit and halter top.

Stupid hormones are what
they should be called, as I resist
knocking her into the next century
today.

*"Oh Mom. Did my lil brother Kevin
call? I have to talk to Davon and Brian
is bringing me home from school today
because I have to handle my business.
Oh, guess what? I'm the manager
for the Varsity Girl's Basketball team."*

Now tell me, what exactly does a manager do,
if she doesn't coach and she doesn't play?
I'm counting to keep from
saying this sounds like so much
manure paper.

When She triumphantly announces that She
is the undisputed freshman Math Star—
certificate of proof in hand.

And the lile girl who ran her tricycle into an unfinished brick wall
and ripped half of her face off, without ever shedding a tear; saying only
"Mommie it hurts—fix me!" The lile girl who walked herself through the longest, ugliest
divorce imaginable: The lil girl who survived her Mother's homelessness,
unemployment, under-employment, 15 hour a day work schedules and plane flights to
almost everywhere together: That lile girl who watched her Mother Tap Dance with
Death and survive this summer, peers through my big girl's eyes, gives me a big hug and
says, *"Don't worry—the apple doesn't fall far from the tree: That's an example of
existentialism Mommie!"* and sashayes her 14 year old butt out of the room.

RETURN TO GOREE: OR THE BRIDE
(for the Fulani Prince without kingdom)

Quand je marche sur la
tombe de ma grand-mère,
Je pleure là où elle et ma mère
Se tenaient—séparées l'une de l'autre,
Le gemissement des pierres,
parmi le beton,
Répond.
un mélange de sang et de corps
Non pa une citadelle Haïtienne
mais un chateau d'esclaves.

"Regardez Gorèe. . .
Ndaaree Gorèe
Voyez-vous ce que vous avez fait?"

J'ai mal comme les femmes
venues ici avant moi,
Je deviens l'ombre
du vent et de l'écume,
des ondes sonores m'emportent, parlent
du passé,
de présent et de ce qui ne peut jamais être.
Mes pied bougent, battent le sol:
Levez la tête,
Mama. . .Toynee hoore ma nden Neene.

La pancarte dit
"Ici les esclaves révoltés
furent pacifiés"
C'est une petite cave à la
taille d'un enfant
minuscule sous l'escalier
montant aux chamres
élégantes des négriers.

"Avez-vous le courage. . ."
Demande-t-il.
"Pouvez-vous voir votre histroire
comme moi qui ai découvert mon visage
dans ceux de ces Africains

dont la fortune est le prix
de ta captivité?"

Walking on my
Grandmother's grave
I howl where she and my mother
stood—separated
Stone cries over hammered
cement
Answers
mixed with blood and bone:
Not Haitian Citadel
but castle of Slaves.

"Regardez Gorèe
Ndaaree Gorèe
See what you have done?"

Aching like the women here
before me,
I become a ghost
of wind and sea foam
riding sound waves of what
was
is now and can never be.
My feet move, thrashing
Levez la tête,
Mama . . .Toynee hoore ma nden Neene.

The sign says
"here is where the rebellious
slaves were calmed."
It is a tiny cave up to my
waist
under the grandstairway
winding its way to the
elegant rooms of the slavers.

"Have you the courage. . ."
He asks.
"Can you see your history
as I have seen my face
reflected in the faces of Africans

who grew rich from your capture?"

Froid, enseveli dans les ténèbres,	Cold, entombed in darkness
Je suis la folie, fille de la perte,	I am the madness born of loss,
là où la première génération	where the first generation
de femmes africanines en déroute	of lost African women
fit un voeu: de s'aimer	would vow to love each other
A travers les temps	across time
A travers l'espace	across space
A travers la folie.	across insanity.

Une peau de cuir, tendue
sur des os fissurés,
moulés à chaud comme un
fil d'or en filigrane;
Une sculpture
de laquella na naîtra aucun fils.

Skin drawn against cracked bone,
to be molded like hot filigree gold;
A sculpture
from which no son will rise.

Les phases de la lune convergent
de même que le sang des
femme fleurissantes converge,
au même moment
sur le meme endroit.
Des rivières de tissue et de sang
couvert le sol
et les hommes
comme l'écume dans le vent
brûlent
dissipent
la premier enfant de ma mère
avant qu'il ne puisse connaître la douleur.

The phases of the moon converge
as the blood flowering of the
women converges together
at the same time
in the same place.
Rivers of tissue and blood
covering the floor
and the men
like blown Sea Foam
churning hot
dissipating
my mother's first child
before it can know pain

"Elegua ouvre la porte . . .
Elegua aan, uddit damal ngal."

"Elegua ouvre la porte. . .
Elegua aan, uddit damal ngal."

Changeant de corps,
J'aperçois l'Atlantique
d'un vaste balcon d'oisiveté
et de pouvoir né de la terreur.
Ma voix devient elle-même
et je chante

Changing bodies,
I see the Atlantic
from the wide balcony of leisure
and power born of terror.
My voice becomes its own
and I sing

   en hurlant, en poussant des
cries d'animaux,
    en fredonnant une
berceuse du Mississippi.

   in whooping yelling
animal noises
   in between crooning a
Mississippi Lullabye.

Le couloir tourne, remonte en spirale	The passage turns, spiraling
de nombreux siècles noirs,	down through so many dark centuries
s'ouvre sur "La Porte Grande Ouverte,"	spilling into "The Open Door"
me dévisage comme	staring at me like
un boogie man amalgamé,	an amalgamated boogie man
qui danse le Jancanou sur mes paupières;	dancing Jancanou on my eyelids;
pendant que tant de cannes de sucre	while so much sugar cane
cinglent mon corps	is brushed over my body
et tracent de petites coupures de rasior	leaving tiny invisible razor
invisibles.	cuts.
Je saigne encore une fois.	I bleed again.
Voilà la mort	It is the death
que je désire	that I want
d'une voix plaidante et adulatrice	in pleading tones of adulation
Je cherche ma grand-mêre	reaching for my grandmother
A portée de bras	an arm's length away
"Je t'aime; je suis ici," dit-il. . .	"Je t'aime; je suis ici," he says. . .
Mido yidi ma, ko doon ngon-mi.	Mido yidi ma, ko doo ngon mi.
Voilà donc	And there
sur "La Porte Grande Ouverte,"	at "The Open Door"
pour me rappeler	to call me back
se montre le fils	is the son of my ancient
abandonné du mari de ma	mother's husband
mère ancestrale	who was left behind

Le Prince de Fulani
   sans royaume,

The Fulani Prince
   without kingdom,

Et avec la gentillesse	And with the gentleness
d'un amour longtemps cheri,	of a long treasured love,
onme ramène à Goree	I am brought back to Goree
où je revendique ce qui est à moi.	to reclaim what is mine.

French Translation in collaboration with Titus Suck

SOUND HAIKU: 5-7-5

forest green smoothness
ignites firefly light trilling
in a tapped toe

too agile to flee
the onslaught of mystery lost
she waits patiently

moody blues thumps now
savagely laconic on
lost love's tears brass door

too hurt salvaging
self, she found her way crying
possibilities

movement too intense
to hold in logic's time such
winsome noise as dance

extra-terrestrial
leaps into space cross bridges
of no return there

I was asked to find
the dangerous part of a
woman and kill it

myself blends raging fire
invincibility with
you to be a girl

JOYCE SCOTT HAIKU
(from "Kicking It With the Old Masters" Exhibit Suite)

Shiva's passion a
wakes to purple being in
world not Buddha

the three temptations
obstructing evolution
movement in mind body

no daddy ever came
home to say goodnight or to
beat my mother blue

Gede attends Day
of the Dead to celebrate
the spirit of the dance

his mission today
from the High God is to a
cemetery rise

bones connect to the
flesh and flesh is connected
to the spirit house

gates of hell open
with Cerebus barking at
ghosts of men who lied

THE EYE OF CARL CLARK: A PHOTOPOEM

I have known rivers
traversed marginal dimensions of
interstellar being to see myself in
    African faces Diaspora wide with
    the kind of white
    that only our teeth can be.
    Men checkmated on Greenmount Avenue
    by perfect black almond eyes
    perplexed in the ecstasy
    of the humor that belies life.
    Nigeria in full motion, with
    a republic of children in Oshogbo
    on Oshun's golden river bordering
    women and men on Mama's Porch
    laughing in purple nights
    beyond the faraway
    non-synchronous music of white lights
    and Metallica subway dreams
    re-spinning potential "Dutchman" scenarios
    where the white woman
    and the black man live together
    in a life
    emanating from head-phoned
    young women altering reality.
    The poetic vocabulary of
    a man in a hat sleeping
    under Frank Sinatra in a hat
    gleaming.
    A boy that looks like a child
    in a uniform,
    celebrants one and all
    on "I Am An American Day."
    We are all Americans I say to
    re-drawn Nubian princesses in hats
    drumming African Methodists Episcopal
    ancestors in "Sunday Go to Meeting" clothes.
    Adorned in printed head-wraps
    hand-woven curled straw brims
    embroidered skull-caps
    molded fabric and white feathers,
    they are Afro-Chic in
    crowns of honor

heralding the ancient beauty
of the sculptured nose
such will-read-you eyes
kissed cheek bones
and the look that breathes
holy, holy, holy
on Sunday and throughout the week.
Though, a turn of the hand will reveal
    the oxymoron of war in pastoral scenes;
    a severed foot on a battlefield of flowers
    a mind wandering space unknown
    between the trees.
    Historic acts captured
    in a moment of violence
    a moment of peace
    in the faces of those
    whose decisions mark
    our time. I have known rivers:
And I sing a world to come as
I walk a world unfathomed
negotiating the rise of Jesus from the dead
crusted in the bucolic acts
of the innocent
whose inner beauty
was filtered pure
by my eye.

                Easter Sunrise 2000

PSALM TO WHAT IS SPIRITUAL IN EACH OF US

sing
"We are the communion of two spirits
journeying into no man's land
at this level of reality.
We are spirits unto ourselves
representing for away places and long ago times.
We are past, present and future
in all of its forms.
We are the motion by which all life develops
expands and dies;
only to develop and expand again.
We are the children. . ."

(Turn to the East)
This word is a song of making
a weaving word of truth
that sees the dark and light side
of ourselves beside ourselves.

(Turn to the West)
This word calls the Peace of
Time to give us a Strength of Will
to do what must be done
to regain the order of Being.

(Turn to the North)
This word is a prophecy
of Prosperity and Health
and Courage to walk in all the dark places
you must go.

(Turn to the South)
This word sounds endlessly through
the generational line carrying us
as it breaks every blood curse
represented in force to bind the
Goodness in us all.
                      This word is I AM.

Index of Poems by Subject Matter

Africa:
  55 Afrikaner—Part I

Alcoholism:
  97 House Made of Dawn

Art:
  112 Joyce Scott Haiku

Blues Poem:
  99 Chanson D'Amour Creole

Class Issues:
  45 Grateful For Shelter
  53 Warnings: Los Angeles Riots
  96 A Black History Month Poem

Dance:
  23 Mother Africa Dance

Driving:
  46 Driving At the Speed of Life

Drugs:
  52 Leaving Suburbia

Erotica:
  12 Why A Lazy Woman Loathes Leaving Her Bed
  79 Conversation
  82 His Eyes Talk
  84 A Ghetto Girl's Love Song
  86 Sometimes It Ain't All About Sex
  98 I Thought He Was A Plant
  103 Alien Pussy

Family:
  20 In My Sista's House
  32 Fishin
  38 Breakfast On 12th Street
  83 7 Years Later
  97 House Made of Dawn
  107 The Daughter Chronicles: Things Her Bad Butt Did

FRIENDSHIP:
- 25 Some People In My Life
- 26 Dania
- 69 In Search of Rainbows
- 78 Poinsettias

GUNS:
- 47 Nick Of Time

HAIR:
- 64 To Understand Is To Understand

HISTORICAL PERSPECTIVES:
- 39 These Are Some of My Blues
- 42 Why I Remember King
- 57 Too Cool Reflections on the Double Digit Double Helix
- 66 I Wanna Tell My Babies
- 85 Ode To Weequaic Heights
- 90 Under Flower: The 1983 March On Washington
- 93 MLK
- 105 JFK, Jr's Last Flight
- 108 Return To Goree: Or The Bride
- 113 The Eye of Carl Clark: A Photopoem

LOVE RELATIONSHIPS:
- 15 Because
- 16 Sunday Morning Orange Juice
- 27 A Prelude to A Time
- 28 Spaces
- 29 When All Else Fails Write Him A Poem
- 30 While We Wait
- 68 Conditions
- 70 Before We Heal
- 71 Truth Don't Need A Name
- 79 Conversation
- 80 Peacock
- 81 Abstract
- 94 La Danse Du Dragon
- 99 Chanson D'Amour Creole
- 102 A Date With Destiny
- 108 Return to Goree: Or The Bride

Mental Health:
- 41 Untitled
- 49 Artificial Light
- 51 Lethargy
- 59 The Peace Poem
- 67 Untitled #1002
- 77 Song #222
- 111 Sound Haiku 5-7-5

Music:
- 10 My Mother Gave me Music

Poet's Craft:
- 35 Ode to the Spoken Word Weavas & Divas
- 36 Cherish The Times
- 60 On Becoming An Artist
- 62 Nosey Lady Lament
- 72 Leo Sun, Scorpio Moon, Cancer...Rising-1
- 92 Forbidden Fruit

Prejudice:
- 65 Perceptions

Spirituality:
- 73 Miami Beach
- 88 Psalms 139:14
- 115 Psalm To What Is Spiritual In Each Of Us

Violence Against Women:
- 22 A Call to Action On A New day Dawning for Naomi
- 54 For Carlotta Who Died at the Age of 20

Womanhood Issues:
- 13 Untitled
- 21 A Maze Groove
- 18 I AM A Mansion
- 34 The Women Gather
- 72 Leo Sun, Scorpio Moon, Cancer...Rising-1
- 76 1994
- 87 Then There Are Times
- 91 La Fleur Haitienne
- 106 La Femme Du Dragon: A Choreopoem

THE AUTHORS

LENETT NEFERTITI ALLEN

Lenett Nefertiti Allen is a literary innovator whose work is distinguished by her spiritual presence, authenticity and humor. She holds the vision of fostering appreciation for literature by presenting it in a context that people from all fabrics of life can appreciate. She manifests her inspiration by weaving poetry, prose, music, hip hop, truth and ritual into word/sound presentations and collaborations with artists around the world. She creates "vis-lit" arts installations using principles of feng shui to conjure sacred space experiences. She has also taught reading-challenged teens and adults how to design their lives through the power of the word via residencies with the Ripken Reading Center, Liberty Medical Center and Baltimore Homeless Union. Her work has been featured in the CSN-TV special *Voices of Our Past*, Theatre Project's *Diverse Works*, Artscape, *Jazzoetry*, and published most recently in the *MD Poetry Review, Poetry Baltimore*, and *Thy Mother's Glass I*. She is the subject of the award-winning video documentary *Mbele Ache*. Between projects, Lenett travels the Earth on behalf of world peace and children. She is a member of the *Trail of Dreams* which walked the Appalachian Mountains in 2000 to honor the visions of our African and Native descendant ancestors.

On a personal tip, she says: "*I see my work as a chronicle of a spiritual being having the human experience of woman of color, mother, daughter, artist, wife, friend... Hopefully, my truth informs the collective human experience with something beautiful, rich and enduring for 7 generations to come. And, to The Almighty be the glory. Aho!*"

LINDA JOY BURKE

Ms. Burke has been writing for 30 years and is the president of the Baltimore Writers Alliance and the poet in residence at the Howard County Center for African American Culture. She has performed at readings sponsored by Enoch Pratt Library, HOCOPOLITSO, the Howard County Library, the National Poetry Therapist Conference, The Association of Women in Psychology Conference and a variety of other venues in the Mid-Atlantic Region. As a workshop leader in developing creativity, she has worked with a cross-section of children and adults in formal classroom and informal community settings. She has appeared in cable access programs about poetry all over the mid-Atlantic region. Selections from her audio collection **"Moods, Minds, and Multitudes"** have been aired on radio stations in the

Baltimore/Washington area and in the Pacific Northwest. Her work is also included in the *Word Up Baltimore* CD and the Howard County Poetry and Literature Society invitational reading series recordings.

On the personal tip she says, *"I believe that through deep personal exploration and integration of the arts into our lives, in whatever form "art" presents itself to us, we are able to enhance our growth and inform our knowing about ourselves and the world more completely. This allows us to heal wounds and create a culture that bridges the best and worse of our history with the best and worst of our possible destiny."*

JAKI-TERRY

Ms. Terry has been a poet since age 6. She was 15 when she started to take her work seriously. Born Lorane Jacqueline Asher on Monday, August 13, 1956 in Wichita Falls, Texas, the eldest of six siblings, she grew up in Cherry Hill (South Baltimore) and attended Baltimore City Public Schools and eventually moved to Newark, New Jersey, where she lived for 12 years. Ten years ago, she came back to Baltimore and acquired The Café MonTage and transformed it into the TLC/The last (poetry) Café, which is now closed. Since then, she has performed up and down the east coast as an accomplished actor, solo performance poet and collectively with her brothers in the revolution, *Black Beret*. Center Stage, Artscape, National State of the Race Conference, Homicide: the television series, and Lollapalooza are just a partial list of her credits.

On a personal tip, she says, *"I'm divorced with no children to personally speak of; yet, I'm momma to many. Although 95-98% of my life I am a practicing vegetarian, it's those occasional cravings for a chicken wing, or steamed crabs (with plenty of Old Bay), or a good piece of lake trout from The Roost that I'm still moving through (smile). I love the mountains, Miami Beach, music from Monk to Maxwell—from Prince to Dead Can Dance. I love children, elders who pass on the lessons, and strong affirming Black Men who love, protect & respect Black Women. Aside from that, I'm just an ordinary "round-the-way-girl," who has come to know that dreams and reality are really just a matter of perspective. Magical, wouldn't you say?"*

CHEZIA THOMPSON CAGER

Dr. Thompson is a Maryland State Arts Council Individual Artist Award recipient for 1999 and 2001, a 1996 Artscape Poetry competition winner (selected by Josephine Jacobsen), and the new director of *Spectrum of Poetic Fire—the Reading Series* at The Maryland Institute, College of Art in Baltimore. Recently she completed and performed "The Joyce Scott Suite Poems" as a tour of "Kicking it with the Old Masters" at the Baltimore Museum of Art. Her most recent poems appear in *Baltimore Review* Winter 2000 and *WordWrights Magazine* July, 2000 and March/April 2001. Her most recent book *The Presence of Things Unseen: Giant Talk* is available through Maisonneuve Press. Her most recent article *"Folk Realities and Bourgosie Fantasies: 4 African-American Artists in Baltimore"* appears in Volume Four of *LINK: A Critical Review of the Arts in Baltimore and the World.* As the subject of the film "PraiseSong for Katherine Dunham: A Choreopoem" she sees her curatorial work as having the same goals as her directorial work at the Mildred E. Bastian and The Mendenhall Centers for the Performing Arts. As the Artscape 2000 Fine Arts Market Curator, her recent exhibits include "Carl Clark: Photographer", " Through the Fire to the Limit—African American Artists in Maryland" and "Playing in the Dark Tower—Images from the Black Literary Landscape." A graduate of Washington University and Carnegie-Mellon University, she has done research studies in Nigeria, Jamaica, and Haiti.

On the personal tip she says, *"I'm a River Maiden, who gives thanks for the gift of love and the mission begun long ago by my maternal grandmother, Mississippi poet and performance artist Mary Ellen Gideon—whose unpublished messages I carry."*

WHEN DIVAS LAUGH combines the chanting of a love goddess, the lessons of a teacher, the warnings of a revolutionary, and the insight of an egungun in the most lyrical poetic song to be sung in years. Maryland/Washington, DC, Texas/New Jersey, and Missouri/Mississippi converge in an apex of powerful voices that don't compete for individual attention but rather they create new spaces to celebrate the century past, while heralding the century to come. A must read and a must hear experience!

For more information email: spectrum@mica.edu